# WORD TO THE WISE

Mark Broatch is a journalist, critic and author, and an unashamed language nerd. An MA (Hons) graduate in English Literature and Linguistics at the University of Auckland, he has been a senior editor and chief subeditor at three national publications in NZ. He is the author of *In a Word, From Airy-Fairy to Yummy Mummy* and *Get the Net* (with Stephen Stratford).

# WORD TO THE WISE

## Untangling the mix-ups, misuse and myths of language

### MARK BROATCH

EXISLE
PUBLISHING

First published 2018

Exisle Publishing Pty Ltd
PO Box 864, Chatswood, NSW 2057, Australia
226 High Street, Dunedin, 9016, New Zealand
www.exislepublishing.com

A CiP record for this book is available from the National Library of Australia.

ISBN 978-1-77559-354-6

Designed by Nick Turzynski of redinc. book design
Typeset in Garamond 12/16
Printed in China

This book uses paper sourced under ISO 14001 guidelines from well-managed forests and other controlled sources.

10 9 8 7 6 5 4 3 2 1

For R and G

# Contents

# How to use this book

This is a book of confusables, words that are misused, misunderstood or questionably employed instead of other words. *Word to the Wise* groups words alongside others with which they are commonly or occasionally confused. Not all confusion occurs as a result of close sounds being muddled, however. Sometimes meanings are swapped or mistaken because words look alike, echo the consonants or vowels of other words or often appear in the same context. Take tortuous and torturous, froideur and hauteur, détente and entente cordiale, malicious and pernicious, cheesy and corny. All appear together here because of how they are used. If a word doesn't appear under its letter, consult the index at the end of the book.

Use is often disputed. Traditionalists say this is the rule and always will be. Free-rolling descriptivist types say you can't control how people use language and I'm not playing by your rules. Dictionaries will tell you that this is where that word came from, what it used to mean and how it's used now. Traditionalists say that's not what I learned and to change it is to risk complete communication breakdown.

The truth is in the middle. Most people use language as they use it, are aware that conventions exist and know — or think they know — one or two well, but are mostly hazy on the rest. *Word to the Wise* presents current usage and offers, when it's helpful, a view of whether any conventions stand up to logic and to how most people are speaking and writing.

Pronunciation aid is given in square brackets. For those who know nothing about phonetic notation, sounds are shown rather than the International Phonetic Alphabet — except for the mid-central vowel sound sometimes called the schwa, which is written as 'ə' and pronounced like the 'a' in 'about'. The book defaults to British usage, and where US usage, pronunciation or spelling is different — some Canadian differences may arise — this is noted. North Americans, Irish and Scots should also note that the suggestions given are non-rhotic — most mid and final 'r's' are not pronounced.

# How to write what you mean to say

No single book can teach you how to write. Becoming a good writer — and in the age of social media we are all writers — is a process of learning and thinking, of writing, of rewriting and, perhaps most of all, of reading. You must read to improve your writing, and you must read the best writers to keep improving. There are no unbreachable rules of writing. But there are things to do and things not to do.

The first thing to do is have a plan. Why are you writing? What's your purpose, your goal? Every essay, blog post, official letter or report requires its own language, style and tone. As part of your plan, have a one-sentence summary of what the piece of writing is intended to achieve — what's sometimes in journalism called a nut graf — and always keep it in front of you, or at least in mind, while you are writing.

A second rule is to answer this question: who's your audience? How will you attract and keep their attention? Will it be the power of your argument, your ability to sway their emotions? To win their attention, they have to trust you. To do this, you must appeal to them using language that is familiar to them, use their frames of reference, the way they relate to the world. We do this all the time when we're speaking to people, to our boss, a child, a stranger or a friend. We automatically adjust our style between conversations, changing our modes of address, our vocabulary. This doesn't mean a writer fakes it, just that they find common ground. They don't patronise, don't make reading harder for their audience by using jargon, obscure words or poorly crafted sentences.

# Think first

To write clearly you need to think clearly. Amazon boss Jeff Bezos, at time of writing the richest man in the world, has reportedly banned PowerPoint or bullet point presentations of ideas. In an email to his senior team, he wrote that those presenting ideas would be required to compose 'narrative' memos of four to six pages, using coherent sentences and clear arguments. They then would read the memo aloud and answer questions. This approach, he said, would force better thinking and understanding of what's important and how things are related. Slide presentations allow speakers to gloss over ideas and gaps in knowledge. Anyone who's listened to a poor presentation with the speaker clicking away at the screen knows the truth of this.

Presenting an idea well — getting readers to buy in — requires clear thinking, coherent ideas and precise expression. How to get there?

## START WITH A BANG

*The cradle rocks above an abyss, and common sense tells us that our existence is but a brief crack of light between two eternities of darkness.*
VLADIMIR NABOKOV

*I have more than once in my time woken up feeling like death. But nothing prepared me for the early morning in June when I came to consciousness feeling as if I were actually shackled to my own corpse.*
CHRISTOPHER HITCHENS

*Every journalist who is not too stupid or too full of himself to notice what is going on knows that what he does is morally indefensible.*
JANET MALCOLM

*Fiction has an entrepreneurial element, akin to the inventor's secret machine, elixir or formula.*
JAMES WOOD

*Saccharine is our sweetest word for fear: the fear of too much sentiment, too much taste.*
LESLIE JAMISON

However you start, grab your reader. Grab them and don't let go. Even if there is no magic formula for writing well, there are tried and true approaches to finding the right ingredients. Limit the number of ideas in sentences, be active rather than passive, be positive, and avoid monotony by mixing up the length, shape and rhythm of sentences. Some can be tight, others looser, depending on your subject and intent.

Be precise and concise. This doesn't mean ideas and their expression are sketched so simply that you leave out important detail, but that you make every word, every sentence count. You can be economical without sacrificing accuracy.

Write with nouns and verbs. This doesn't mean no adjectives or adverbs, but they must help a sentence's precision and economy rather than make it flabbier. Prefer the short word to the long, the simple to the complex, the concrete to the abstract. Concrete language demands less of the reader than abstract. Sometimes you need abstract ideas to convey complex ideas, but usually it's best to use tangible concepts, graspable metaphors, real-world examples.

Don't be afraid to keep things simple. Sometimes people overcomplicate sentences because they are afraid of looking stupid. But don't be fearful of complex sentences. If they are clear, they can illuminate the toughest subjects.

Mix up the order of your sentences so that they have punch at their start and end. Rather than always using a simple subject-verb-object structure — 'The skipper made one last attempt to rescue the man from the rocks as the tide rose and the waves crashed higher' — switch the sentence around. 'As the tide rose and the waves crashed higher on the rocks, the skipper made one last attempt to rescue the stranded, exhausted man.' Don't be afraid to start sentences with conjunctions such as but, and, although or so, especially if the sentences are tightly linked. 'Proust must be cited for his notion of the "musical" structuring of memories (the task of narrating having been equated with the task of remembering). But, of course, there are predecessors.' (Susan Sontag).

Avoid clichés and stale metaphors. Limit the use of passive language; it can make your writing impersonal and drain it of life, because the passive shifts focus from the doer of the action to the action itself. The classic example of this is the CEO who says 'mistakes were made'. But using the passive might be appropriate if you are writing for a scientific or bureaucratic audience, or don't actually want to admit making a mistake.

Choose plain, direct words (give, tender, sudden, thief) over long Latinate words full of prefixes and suffixes. Nominalisations — nouns made from adjectives and verbs — are particularly disliked by traditionalists and admirers of good writing. Like passive language, they drain your writing of precision and power and can conceal who's doing what to whom. But they are used widely, and not just by academics, lawyers and bureaucrats, because of that reason. Keep in mind that English has been nouning and verbing for centuries. Perhaps because they are associated with the hype of business, a few attract particular scorn, including impact, leverage, action, task and grow (as of a company).

Even if many of the language conventions and preferences are based on little more than superstition, knowing them will give you confidence. Lack of confidence, or fear of looking a fool, has tripped up many a writer. They reach for the fanciest words, turn everything into a passive voice to sound authoritative, follow half-understood prohibitions from childhood lessons and end up sounding flat and pompous — and nothing like themselves. Learn the 'rules'. Your confidence will be redoubled if you know the conventions that most often light the touchpaper of traditionalists and can veer around them.

*In writing you can always change the ending or delete a chapter that isn't working. Life is uncooperative, impartial, incontestable.*
ARIEL LEVY

## REWRITE, REWRITE, REWRITE

Professional writers emphasise that the real writing is done in the rewriting. Nothing is finished in one draft. They go over each sentence and paragraph dozens of times, sometimes more.

Asked about how much rewriting he did, Hemingway famously replied, 'It depends. I rewrote the ending to *Farewell to Arms*, the last page of it, 39 times before I was satisfied.' What was the problem, asked the interviewer. Said Hemingway: 'Getting the words right.'

Other writers rewrite to 'relax' the prose because the first draft tends to be rather uptight. Even Lee Child, who does only one draft of his 100 million-selling Jack Reacher thrillers, admits to 'combing' through his writing of the day before, 'smoothing' out only a little before carrying on.

The phrase 'kill your darlings' has been attributed to William Faulkner, Stephen King, Allen Ginsberg, even Anton Chekov. Probably the first person to use it — though he may have been paraphrasing Samuel Johnson — was English critic Sir Arthur Quiller-Couch. He meant ridding your writing of extraneous ornament, not letting anything below-par get past. It is writing — clever phrases, lovely but pointless metaphors, repetition of the argument, pieces of filler writing that the eyes slip past without any adhesion — that doesn't advance the whole. Killing your darlings means being an editor rather than a writer.

## THESAURUS OR NOT?

What makes us think writing is of the highest quality? Cognitive psychologist Steven Pinker says two of the features that 'distinguish sprightly prose from mush' are a varied vocabulary and the use of unusual words. But this can go horribly wrong. You can end up using the most arcane, least appropriate words, and end up not saying what you mean to say. Your writing will sound forced, and you might come across as try-hard. Remember that the thesaurus, as one English professor said, is 'a good reminder of words momentarily forgotten, but a bad guide to words previously unknown'. Use it to find the words on the tip of your tongue, not words you've never heard of. Words have core senses but also connotations and phonesthetics — how the sound of words influences meaning. As another wise person noted, use a thesaurus at the end of writing, not the beginning.

> *A line will take us hours maybe;*
> *Yet if it does not seem a moment's thought,*
> *Our stitching and unstitching has been naught.*
> W.B. YEATS

# The right tone

A piece of writing should feel natural, despite all the editing and rewriting work you've put in. It should sound in your voice, but your very best voice, your smartest and most eloquent. The tone of voice, or register, should be appropriate to your audience. Society has become more relaxed. The latest generation are adept at switching registers between a text, email, chat, blog post. But be careful when moving between mediums that you don't carry the casual language and style of social media into an essay, a report, a work-related email:

> *Yo bro, what's the haps with those reports, they were due yesterday, I can't even #wtf*

# A few common errors

Terrible, isn't it, that previous sentence. It uses a comma splice, which links two independent clauses with a comma where a full stop, semi-colon or a conjunction such as and or but might be more suitable. Even writers and editors who raise an eyebrow at stuffy language rules often dislike them.

Yet, as with many conventions, you can ignore the prohibition on the comma splice if you are good or famous enough. Samuel Beckett, Somerset Maugham and E.M. Forster were all users of the comma splice.

Even the sternest language guides say comma splices are okay when the clauses are short and balanced and the tone is conversational. 'Easy come, easy go', for example. Comma splices are common, and perfectly at home, on social media, which mimics patterns of speech far more than most writing. But in more formal contexts, comma splices might appear casual, careless or unprofessional. Avoid them particularly combined with conjunctions such as however. 'Productivity gains are inevitable given the level of investment, however many positions are likely to become surplus to requirements.'

## DON'T DANGLE

Dangling participles in particular annoy many traditionalists, perhaps because, once you have attuned yourself to them, they seem so silly and illogical. Participles of verbs are often used in subordinate clauses that introduce sentences. They must refer to the main subject of the sentence.

'Finding the path, the wood quickly became impassibly thick.' This is wrong, because it is saying the wood found the path. It would need to be something like: 'Finding the path, the hiker entered the wood, which quickly became impassibly thick.'

But sentences can dangle in other ways, always with the introducing subordinate clauses left hanging.

Don't write: 'At age 60, her teachers still thought she had a decade of singing in her.' Or this: 'An epic venture, Jane Brown went to the lengths of including all of her extended family's portraits in a collage that delivered a one-two hit of warmth and poignancy.' That last one is a close copy of a real one, which went through a real subeditor.

Many of the words in this book are commonly confused. This is often because writers have only a vague idea of what they mean, or they think they mean something that they don't.

If you are not sure of the meaning, check it. If you are using words whose meaning has shifted or is disputed — nonplussed, disinterested, moot, shibboleth — make sure your intent is clear through context.

# End well

*I hoped for my cousin to fail, and wished him luck.*
JOHN JEREMIAH SULLIVAN

*The breeze is the merest puff, but you yourself sail headlong and breathless under the gale force of the spirit.*
ANNIE DILLARD

*And I'm thinking about our prison cell — I hope it's not too small — and beyond its heavy door, worn steps ascending: first sorrow, then justice, then meaning. The rest is chaos.*
IAN MCEWAN

*If Harold Bloom continues to devote his life to the hopeful proposition that ordinary readers, as much as players and scholars, may become free artists of themselves, then good luck to him. He's only human.*
ANTHONY LANE

How you end a piece of writing is important too. It's the payoff, the thank you, for spending time with what has taken the writer far longer to compose than it took you to read. It should give the reader something to ponder, or leave them wanting more.

# A-Z OF
# CONFUSED
# AND
# MISUSED
# WORDS

To **abrogate** [ab-roh-gate] is to end or abolish something, particularly in an official or formal manner, or to evade, particularly a responsibility. To **arrogate** [a-roh-gate] is to take or claim something, such as a right, without justification. To **derogate** [de-roh-gate] is to disparage or insult; (*derogate from*) to detract from; (*derogate from*) to deviate from expectations. A **surrogate** [suh-ro-gət] is a substitute, a deputy, or a woman who carries and gives birth to a child for another.

A theory or topic under discussion is **abstruse** if it's difficult to understand, from the Latin for 'put away' or 'hidden'. People are sometimes called **obtuse** if they are slow to understand or insensitive to others' feelings. Obtuse, which comes from the Latin for 'to beat against', also means blunt in a technical sense, so refers to an angle that's more than 90° but less than 180°. Because of the 'ob' prefix, it might be confused with **obverse**, which means 'turns toward'. The obverse is the opposite side of a fact or truth, or the logical counterpart of a proposition. It's also the side of a coin or medal that bears the principle design (the other side is the **reverse**); serving as an opposite or counterpart; facing the observer. Reverse generally means the opposite or contrary, or having the back of something showing to the observer.

As a verb it means to exchange the positions of, or to move or drive or cause to function in the opposite way. **Perverse**, which is often used as a mild insult, means contrary in nature, in deliberate opposition to what's expected, desired or reasonable.

Something that is **abysmal** is extremely bad (*an abysmal film*), or very great or severe (*abysmal poverty*), or — occasionally — might refer to resembling an abyss, i.e. a very deep chasm. **Abyssal** usually refers to an abyss or the bottom layers of the ocean. It can be used to mean immeasurable, unfathomable.

To **accede** to something is to agree (*accede to a request*), or to take office (*acceded to the throne*). To **exceed** is to go beyond something, such as a target, limit or budget. To **succeed** is to achieve or do well, or to take office after someone leaves the position.

To **accept** is to approve, generally agree upon or to receive. To **except** is to leave out, and also is a preposition for excluding or only. An **excerpt** is a short passage or segment taken from a longer work, such as a text, film or musical composition; to excerpt is to take such an **extract.**

A proposal might be deemed **acceptable** to a person or group, but sometimes a sentence will confuse it with **amenable**, such as: *The plan to run trams from the city to the southern suburbs seemed amenable to the council and government.* Amenable describes the party open to the proposal, not the idea. Write instead: *The council was amenable to the plan* or *The plan appeared to be acceptable to the council.*

**Acrimony** is bitterness or animosity, exhibited in speech or actions. **Alimony** is a support allowance paid by one former spouse to another following a divorce. **Antimony** is a metallic white chemical element. **Hegemony** [he-JE-muh-nee but also he-GE-muh-nee and he-je-MOH-nee] is the dominance of one group over others, usually by way of controlling norms and ideas, or the dominant position of a set of ideas that become fixed and 'commonsensical' and so prevent others being disseminated or considered. **Parsimony** is extreme reluctance to spend money, excessive economy. **Sanctimony** is feigned piety or righteousness, the show of being morally superior to others, affected saintliness. **Simony** (a less common term in modern times) is making profit out of selling religious pardons, favours or sacred things. (See **condescending**)

The names of organisations such as NASA (National Aeronautics and Space Administration), inventions such as sonar (*so*und *n*avigation *a*nd *r*anging), chemicals such as GABA (*g*amma *a*mino*b*utyric *a*cid) and groups such as the Gestapo (*Ge*heime *Sta*ats*po*lizei) are true **acronyms** — words formed using the initial letters of other words that can be pronounced as a word. All other words created out of initial letters are properly called **initialisms** (BBC, COPD, GDP). Although an older word, initialism is less known, and the use of acronym to refer to any word formed out of initials is unfortunately common. Some publication style guides stipulate that acronyms should be written as proper nouns, with only an initial capital — Nato, Anzac — apart from those already common nouns or with a few exceptions, such as AIDS, like other initialisms. Some more traditionalist publications still insist that initialisms such as G.D.P. be separated by full stops (periods in the US).

Short sayings that express helpful ideas come in many forms, and there's considerable crossover in how sayings are categorised. An **adage** is a saying, proverb or short statement that has come to be accepted as true over time ('No pain, no gain'). An **aphorism** is a pithy observation believed to contain a general truth ('Power tends to corrupt, and absolute power corrupts absolutely': Lord Acton). In logic or mathematics, an **axiom** is a formal statement that can be used as the basis of further reasoning; it can also be a self-evident or universally accepted principle ('Change is the only constant in life'). A **dictum** is likewise a short statement that expresses a general truth ('Pick your battles'). It is also an authoritative, often formal pronouncement or assertion. (An **obiter dictum** is a judge's expression of opinion on a point not essential to a legal decision.) A **maxim** is a concise, pithy statement that expresses a general truth or rule of conduct, or an aphorism ('All happy families are alike; each unhappy family is unhappy in its own way': Tolstoy). A **motto** is a short phrase intended to reflect the beliefs and intentions of a person, family or institution, especially as accompanying a coat of arms (Adidas's most recent motto is: 'Impossible is nothing'); in music, a motto is a recurring phrase. (See **epigram**)

To **adduce** is to show as evidence or proof (*adduce additional evidence*). To **deduce** is to infer or judge based on what one knows (*nothing more could be deduced*). (See **imply**)

It would seem unlikely that people might confuse a fancy word for saying goodbye with one that means a fuss or bustling confusion, but because both are uncommon in everyday English, the mix-up is not entirely surprising. **Adieu** [ad-yu], which comes from French meaning literally 'to God', is usually either said as an interjection meaning goodbye — 'Adieu!' — or as a parting statement: 'I bid you adieu'. **Ado** is a Middle English variation of 'at do' or 'to do', meaning fuss or trouble, as in 'a to-do about nothing'. It is probably most often used in modern times in the phrase 'Without further ado . . .' in formal speeches, and hence the hypercorrection/pseudo-sophistication instinct probably kicks it into 'Without further adieu . . .'. And no, it's nothing to do with *Hamlet*: 'O, that this too too solid flesh would melt / Thaw and resolve itself into a dew!' (See **myself**, **that** and **which**, **whom**)

**Adverse** events or effects are unfavourable (*adverse conditions contributed to a late start to the race*). **Averse** usually applies to people and means opposed or strongly disinclined to something (*I am not averse to changing my mind on this*).

To give **advice** [-vise] is to offer one's opinion, counsel, recommendation; that is, to **advise** [-vize] them.

An **aesthetic** [ees-thet-ik] judgment is appreciative of, and concerned with the ideas of, art, beauty and good taste. An aesthetic is a set of principles underlying the work of a particular artist or art movement or, more informally, an individual's or group's sense of creative style or taste. An **aesthete** [ees-theet] is a person who affects a strong appreciation of beauty and art. An **ascetic** person is rigidly austere in her or his living habits, often for spiritual reasons, or a person who practises extreme self-denial. (See **austere**)

An **affable** person is friendly, warm and approachable. If something is **ineffable**, however, it is incapable of being expressed in words (*the ineffable wonder of space*) or should not be uttered, such as the name of a deity in some religions.

The near-homonyms **affect** and **effect** confuse many. **Affect** as a verb means to make a difference to something — that is, to have an effect on it (*it affected their work*). It also means to pretend to have or feel something (*to affect a friendship*). The stress is on the second syllable: af-FECT. (Hence **affectation**, which is carefully devised behaviour that's designed to impress or be noticed, though pronounced AF-fectation.) In psychology, an affect is an experience or observable expression of emotion, and the stress is on the first syllable: AF-fect (*he had a flat affect*). An **effect** is a change that comes about as a result of some action, such a result, or the impression in someone's mind (*a pleasant effect*). The stress is on the second syllable: e-FFECT. To effect as a verb is to bring about (*she effected the changes*).

To **aggregate** [ag-rə-GATE] is to gather into a whole. The aggregate [AG-rə-gət] is the whole or total amount. To **congregate** is to gather, assemble. To **segregate** is to separate or isolate from others in a wider group.

To **aid** is to help, to offer assistance of someone or something, particularly of a tangible form; to give such assistance or support; or it constitutes money or supplies from a rich country to a poorer one (*aid budget*); or is something that assists or supports, particularly technology (*teaching aid, hearing aid*). An **aide** is an assistant to an important person, especially a head of government or military leader (*presidential aide*). Or it is someone who assists as they train (*teacher's aide, nurse's aide*).

The **aisle** of a church or supermarket is the passage between the seats or shelves. An **isle** is an island, especially in literary or romantic contexts.

**Alimentary** relates to digestion or food. That which is **elementary** is basic, fundamental or relates to early school in the US.

**Alliteration** is the occurrence of the same letter/s or sound/s at the beginning of a series of words (*a fair few lively lads*). **Assonance** is the occurrence of the same vowel sounds (*the long wrong song*) and is often extended to identical consonants with different vowels (*milled, mulled, mould*). **Consonance** means harmony; agreement; or is the repetition of consonants in series of words, particularly stressed final sounds (*mint scent, a bright breath broth*). **Dissonance** is inharmonious sound, discord or lack of agreement.

**Allusive** means something contains implied or indirect references — i.e. allusions — or refers to something in an indirect way. That which is **elusive** is evasive or difficult to capture, understand or define. Something that's **illusive** is illusory, having the nature of an illusion. (See **delude, delusion**)

To sing **aloud** is to do it audibly. If you are **allowed**, that is — permitted by your landlord.

Is **alright** okay, or should it always be **all right**? Dictionaries and style guides either dislike alright or hedge their bets, suggesting there is nothing to say alright is not acceptable logically. Altogether and already are fine (and always, for that matter), some say, so why the fuss? Ah, but alright means okay or satisfactory, says one argument, while all right means everything was correct. Yet context usually makes meaning clear (*How was the film? It was alright/all right.*) If you want to avoid altercations with traditionalists, it is never considered incorrect to write all right. Or use alright only to mean satisfactory (*he sings alright*) but nowhere else (*everything turned out all right*). If you are writing for a publication or publisher they will have a rule for this, which will almost certainly not be alright. It's inevitable alright will win out in time because English is nothing if not a fan of conciseness.

An **altar** is a ceremonial table in Christian churches and other religious buildings. To **alter** something is to change it, usually in a small way, and especially to change the size or fit of clothes.

To **alternate** [ol-ter-nate] means to do things by turns or to follow on from. Every alternate year is every second one. An **alternative** is another choice or possibility, one of two or more (*an alternative outfit*). It can refer to mutually exclusive options (*Which alternative do you most favour?*). Yet **alternate** and **alternative** are increasingly being interchanged adjectivally, particularly to mean 'another'. In the US in particular, it is common to see written 'alternate route' or 'alternate reality' [ol-ter-net], seeming to use it as the other of two choices. Properly speaking, an alternate reality would be one that followed on from this one in a kind of weird rotation. This newer use, particularly given Google Translate's 'alternate translations', is likely to obliterate the difference in such contexts. Alternative is likely to retain its particular meaning of 'not mainstream', most commonly seen in 'an alternative lifestyle' or 'alternative medicine', and the adverbs might survive for a while yet (*alternatively, you could go by train rather than drive; she worked* *her two jobs as doctor and full-time mother alternately, year on, year off*). Or perhaps alt — alt-right, for example — will eventually be enough for everything. (See **disinterested, fulsome, moot, nonplussed**)

Sometimes understandably muddled are a few words relating to responsibilities and areas of influence. An **ambit** is the extent, sphere or bounds of something (*that goes beyond the ambit of this discussion*). A **remit** is one's area of responsibility or task (*do not venture beyond your remit*). As a verb, remit also means to send money or the sum sent being a remittance, to refrain or pardon, or to refer. **Auspices** [aw-spi-siz], which usually appears in plural, can be confused with these words because it means patronage, sponsorship, protection (*under the auspices of the Department of Internal Affairs*). In ancient Rome the auspex was someone who observed the flight of birds for good omens, and came to mean a protector. Similarly, **aegis** [ee-jis], which came from a shield of the gods, refers to the backing, support or protection of a person or an organisation (*under the aegis of the Vatican*). An **orbit**, meanwhile, is usually the circle around a — typically planetary — body, but also an area of influence (*you don't want to come within her orbit*). (An **obit** is a familiar abbreviation for an obituary, a public notice of a death.) (See **gambit**)

**Ambivalence** was originally a term in psychology for the holding of two contradictory ideas or emotions about someone or something, but now a person who is **ambivalent** might just have mixed feelings or is a little uncertain. If something is **ambiguous**, it has more than one possible meaning or interpretation (*ambiguous statements*) or is not clear (*an ambiguous ending*). (See **cunctation, equivocation, waver**)

A person might be **amiable**: friendly, agreeable, good-natured. A gathering or a social exchange, however, might be **amicable**, being characterised by goodwill.

To be **amoral** is to be not concerned with morality. To be **immoral** or indulge in such behaviour is to act contrary to established moral standards.

There are plenty of less common words for those who don't struggle with a sense of confidence. **Amour propre** [amoor propr], which is French for self-love, is self-esteem, a sense of one's own worth. **Braggadocio** [brag-ah-doh-chee-oh], from a character in a historical play, is boastful, swaggering behaviour. **Chutzpah** [hoots-pah or khoots-pah], from Yiddish, is strong self-confidence or cheekiness, the word usually used positively. **Hubris** [hyoo-briss or hoo-briss] is excessive self-confidence, pride or presumption, usually used negatively. (See **froideur**)

To be **amused** is to be entertained by something funny. Traditionally, to be **bemused** was to be puzzled or confused. But a state of bemusement is now being used to suggest feelings of wry amusement about something, or to be preoccupied or lost in thought. Another one to employ with care. (See **nonplussed**)

A general **anaesthetic** brings about unconsciousness in a patient; local anaesthetic brings about loss of sensation in a small part of the body; regional anaesthetic brings about loss of sensation in a larger part of the body, such as a leg. A **sedative**, meanwhile, is a substance that induces a relaxed state in a patient. (See **sedation**)

We are sometimes a troubled species, or at least self-involved, and words that describe social and existential alienation are not in short supply. Many are borrowed from other languages. **Angst**, from German, is a feeling of deep anxiety or dread; or a feeling of persistent worry, often over something trivial. **Anomie** [an-oh-mee], from Greek via French, traditionally refers to social instability following an absence or breakdown of principles or sense of purpose; it sometimes is also used to refer to an individual's sense of alienation and unease. If you're looking for a word that describes weariness or dissatisfaction resulting from boredom or lack of excitement there's **ennui** [on-wee], from French. Then there's **weltschmerz** [velt-shmehrts], which is a world-weariness, melancholy, sorrow or anxiety about the ills of the world. Because it is recently borrowed from German, the word, meaning 'world + pain', is sometimes employed with a capital letter in that language's tradition. A less common term is **acedia** [a-see-dee-uh] (or accidie [ak-si-dee]), from Greek via Latin, which describes spiritual or mental torpor or apathy, sloth. (See **apathy**)

An **annal**, which is usually in plural, is a yearly record of events (*the annals of the seventeenth century*). Or simply historical records, or figuratively (*it will go down in the annals of history*). To be **annual** is to happen once a year or every year; or living or growing for one year or season. To **annul** is to declare something invalid, such as a marriage. To be **annular**, a less common word, is to be ring-shaped. **Anal** of course means of the anus; it's also a common shortening of 'anally retentive', an informal term that is often applied to people of a particularly meticulous, strict or uptight manner.

To be **anodyne** is to be intentionally inoffensive or harmless, innocuous; or to serve to relieve pain or soothe. To **anodise** is to cover a metal with a coating using electric or chemical means.

Fancy words for times long ago can be used vaguely or incorrectly. **Antebellum** means (often of a style, architecture or attitude) relating to a period before a war, particularly the American Civil War (Latin *ante bellum* = before the war). **Antediluvian** is often used to mean extremely old or ridiculously old-fashioned (Latin *ante dilivium* = before the flood, as described in the Bible). **Prelapsarian** means belonging to the time or state before the moral fall of humankind by Adam and Eve described in the Bible; hence characteristic of any innocent, unspoilt or carefree period (Latin pre lapsus = before the fall).

**Anterior** means to the front, or before in time or place. **Posterior** means to the back, coming after; of a birth it refers to the lower half coming first rather than head; and is an informal term for the buttocks. **Ulterior** means hidden, especially intentionally.

In psychological contexts an **antisocial** person is someone who engages in activities that are reckless, aggressive and potentially harmful to others, whereas if they are **asocial** they avoid, have no interest in or lack the ability to have contact with others. In everyday use someone who doesn't enjoy the company of others is commonly termed **unsociable**. The word **unsocial** is typically applied to working hours that make having a social life difficult. These four words are frequently interchanged, so if there's any chance of confusion it would pay to make your meaning clear through context.

The **antithesis** is the direct opposite of something or someone; an opposition or contrast; a rhetorical contrast of ideas; a proposition that opposes another. A **synthesis** is a converging or unification of elements, substances or ideas. (A **synopsis** is a summarising view.) A **thesis** is a proposition advanced for argument, or a long dissertation written and submitted for a higher degree.

**Apathy** is lack of interest, emotion or willingness to take action. **Lethargy** is the state of being sluggish, drowsy, unenergetic, indifferent, lazy. **Inertia** is resistance or disinclination to action, activity or change, especially when it is desired. In physics it means the resistance of a body to any change in its state of momentum. (See **angst**)

**Apostasy** is the formal abandonment of a religion by a person who once professed to being a believer. Apostates are sometimes shunned, or worse. **Heresy** might precede apostasy. It is an opinion or action at odds with established beliefs, or adherence to such views. A heretic might also be accused of **blasphemy** — an act or attitude that's considered irreverent, insulting or contemptuous of that which is considered religiously sacred. They might be called an **infidel** — a pejorative term for a person who doesn't believe in a religion seen as the true one.

To **appease** is to pacify or attempt to pacify, especially by allowing concessions (*to appease protesters*); to soothe, ease or allay (*appease my conscience*). To **propitiate** is to gain or regain the favour of, or avert the anger or malice of, particularly of a superior being such as a god. That which is **propitious**, meanwhile, is favourable or indicates future success.

To **appraise** is to estimate the worth or significance of something (*Will you appraise this ring, please?*); to check. To **apprise** (of) is to inform or tell, often oneself (*let me apprise you of the latest staff changes*).

**Approbation** is praise, approval or consent. **Opprobrium** is harsh criticism or blame, or public disgrace as a result of shameful or bad behaviour.

To **appropriate** [ə-proh-pree-ATE] is to take possession of something for oneself; or to annex. An appropriate amount [ə-PRO-pree-ut] would be suitable, fitting. To **expropriate** [ex-proh-pree-ATE] is to deprive an owner of property or other things of value, especially for public use; or to transfer someone else's property, especially to oneself.

**Arbitrage** is the practice of simultaneously buying and selling in separate markets to take advantage of differing prices for the same financial asset; to arbitrage is to engage in such activity. **Triage** is the medical sorting of patients by urgency of need, usually in large numbers, or as a verb to decide that treatment order. It also means the assigning of priority order or importance in areas outside of medicine (*security triage*).

An **arc** is a curve or curving path of something, such as a ball or celestial body. It also has related mathematical and electrical meanings, but its most common everyday use is in connection with telling stories: the development or progression of the narrative or an element of it (*the film's dramatic arc; her character's emotional arc*). An **ark** is the boat built by Noah to save his family and the animals from the coming flood, or an ancient wooden box sacred to Jewish belief.

That which is **arrant** nonsense is complete rubbish, without any qualification. The word rarely appears outside of this phrase. To be **errant**, however, is to behave badly, often mentioned in humorous contexts (*an errant wife*); in literary contexts, it can mean travelling or wandering, often appearing after the noun (*knight errant*); or straying, out of the appropriate place (*an errant golf shot*).

Something that's **artful** is clever or skilful, especially if it achieves a result and is done in a sly manner (*artful wording*); or is simply performed with or showing art or skill (*artful direction*). If it's **artless** it is free from guile or artifice (*an artless child*) or without pretentiousness or obvious effort (*seemingly artless technique*). Or it's crude, without finesse (*artless prose*). Be careful you don't send the wrong message. (See **disingenuous**)

To **ascend** is to rise upwards in the air, go up or climb, physically or metaphorically (*ascending the career ladder*). If a path ascends it slopes upwards. An **ascent** is a climb or act of rising, a slope one might climb or walk up, or social or professional progress. To **assent** is to express agreement, particularly after a period of consideration. It is an expression of approval or agreement, often an official one. To **consent** means to agree to something. A consent is an agreement or permission to do something, often formally, such as consent to marry.

To **ascribe** something to something is to attribute, assign a cause. To **describe** is to give an account of it in words. To **inscribe** it is to mark with your signature or words, to engrave or to informally dedicate. To **prescribe** is to specify with authority or formally advise, or to issue a medical prescription. To **proscribe** is to prohibit or make illegal. To

**subscribe** is to receive as a result of regular payment; to subscribe to something is to believe it, as in a theory. To **transcribe** is to write out in full, from notes or another medium, or to convert or rearrange from one form to another.

**Asinine** is idiotic, or resembles an ass. **Inane** means lacking sense, stupid. **Insane**, said of a person, means mentally deranged; said of an idea, say, it means absurd or senseless.

An **ass** is a donkey, an animal in the horse family. Or it's a stupid or obstinate person; the buttocks (impolite, US); or a slightly more polite term for arse (UK). A **mule** is the usually infertile offspring of a male donkey and female horse — a **hinny** is the offspring of a female donkey and male horse.

To **asseverate** is to assert, to declare positively or seriously. To **eviscerate**, literally, is to disembowel, as in to remove the viscera or internal organs. More commonly it is used figuratively to mean to gut — to remove the essential elements of something or deprive of vitality (*he eviscerated his debating opponent*). (See **visceral**)

If you are an **assiduous** sort you don't mind hard work or attention to detail. It also means constant (*assiduous career development*). **Insidious** means beguiling but harmful and spreading (*insidious lies*). To **insinuate** something, on that note, is to suggest or hint, particularly something bad, in an indirect or sly way; to insinuate yourself into something means to manoeuvre yourself into becoming part of something or into a favourable position, using subtle and possibly underhand methods. That which is **invidious** tends to cause resentment, envy or ill will (*an invidious assignment),* or is unfair (*comparisons are invidious*).

To **assure** is to convince, to state positively to someone in attempt to remove doubt, to make certain that something will happen. As well as assuring afresh, to **reassure** is likewise to state positively to try to remove doubt, but also fear, and to inspire confidence (*she reassured her elderly neighbour after the robbery*). To **ensure** is to make sure, certain or secure. To **insure** is to buy or provide insurance cover for; occasionally, to ensure.

Something that is **atavistic** shows resemblance or reversion to something ancient or ancestral, such as a characteristic. It's popularly called a 'throwback'. Because of the sounds in the word it might be confused with **avatar**, a representation of a person, especially in online or computer game environments, or a manifestation in human form. Which is not to be confused with **vicarious** — experienced imaginatively through someone or something else. People often talk about the 'vicarious thrill' of hearing about others' brave or foolish adventures. These might be **visceral** experiences — relating to that which is felt deeply within rather than on the surface or through the intellect. (See **eviscerate**)

To **attenuate** [ə-TEN-yoo-ate] is to reduce, make thin or fine, lessen in amount or severity, weaken. Something that's attenuate [aten-yoo-ət] is reduced or weakened, attenuated. To **extenuate** [ex-TEN-yoo-ate] is to lessen or attempt to lessen the severity or seriousness of something, such as a criminal offence, to mitigate (*extenuating circumstances*).

An **aubade** [oh-bahd] is a morning love song, or a song or poem announcing or celebrating the *dawn* ('The anaesthetic from which none come round', reads a line from Phillip Larkin's cheerlessly fearful offering of the same name). A **nocturne** is a musical composition, in particular evoking or inspired by the *night*, or an instrumental composition of a dreamy nature. To **serenade** is to sing or play music to someone, usually in the open air in the *evening* and often in an attempt to woo them; to entertain in the open air in the evening with music and song, such as diners in a restaurant, or such a performance. It's also a light classical composition of more than one movement.

An **auger** is a tool for boring holes. To **augur** is to predict, be an indication of. In ancient Rome it was an official who interpreted natural signs for indications of divine intent. Don't hear, as some have, 'It all goes well' when 'It augurs well' is said.

An **august** organisation inspires admiration and respect; an august building is majestic and full of grandeur. Something that's **austere**, however, is plain and simple, unadorned to the point of harshness. Such a person is stern and cold, probably morally strict and not given to pleasure. (See **ascetic**)

**Aural** relates to the ears, hearing. **Oral** is spoken rather than written, or relating to the mouth. **Verbal** means concerned with words, but can also differentiate the spoken from the written (*a verbal warning*).

A self-taught person is an **autodidact**, from the Greek. A **polymath**, also from the Greek, is a person whose learning covers a wide range of subjects. (A **polyglot** speaks many languages.) An **opsimath** is a person who studies or learns late in life, while a **philomath** is someone who loves acquiring new knowledge.

To **aver** is to strongly assert or affirm; in legal contexts it means to prove, verify or assert as fact. To **avert** is to keep from happening (avert trouble), or to turn away one's eyes, gaze or thoughts.

In US English, **backward** is both adjective and adverb: a backward glance, a backward somersault; one looks, walks, counts and bends over backward to help someone. If you are moving to the back, rear, past or in reverse, you do it backward. In UK English, **backwards** tends to be the adverb and backward the adjective. So it's a backward glance but a step backwards. A backward step, of course, is usually a regrettably retrograde one. A country can be termed backward in terms of, say, technology, though it is offensive to use it about people's intelligence. A person can be backward, as in shy, about their talents, and 'not backward in sharing his views'. The opposite of this is **forward**, sometimes appearing as the adverb **forwards** in the UK (*the car began to move forwards*), though not in the US. **Afterwards** is common as an adverb in the UK (*they went home shortly afterwards*) but is usually afterward in the US. **Downwards** is probably preferred as adverb in the UK in formal contexts, but downward is at least as commonly used. Toward is preferred as a preposition in the US (*she moved toward him*) but **towards** in the UK. (See **forward**)

If you are waiting with **bated** breath it is in excited or nervous anticipation. Probably because it is rare outside this phrase, it is very commonly written as **baited**, as a hook or trap loaded with bait to catch its target. The word bated is a shortening of abated, first recorded with Shylock speaking in Shakespeare's *Merchant of Venice*: 'Shall I bend low and in a bondman's key, / With bated breath and whispering humbleness, Say this:'

**Baleful** and **baneful** are two archaic, poetically valuable words that are frequently confused because both carry a vague sense of evil or woe. **Bale** is malignant evil, pain or misery. So baleful has the senses of evil or harmful, but also sorrowful. A baleful look traditionally was an ominous or menacing one, holding the potential for violence, but it could also just be gloomy or lugubrious. **Bane** originally signified death or poison, but now means harm, ruin or the source of great distress (*you are the bane of my life*). So baneful means poisonous or destructive. Unless you're a poet, stick to sorrowful versus poisonous and you'll not upset traditionalists. (See **benign**, **lugubrious**)

If the air or the weather is **balmy** it is pleasant and warm. If someone calls you **barmy** (UK slang, often jocular) you are mentally unsound, or at least a little crazy (*that music is driving me barmy*). A barmy idea is a foolish one.

To **bare** is to remove one's clothes or to uncover. It's also naked, uncovered or unadorned. To **bear** is to carry or convey, to support, to endure, to give birth to or to produce, as a plant of fruit or vegetables. It's a large furry mammal too. One's **bearing** is the way a person conducts or holds themselves. Bearing is also relevance (*it has no bearing on our plans*); the relative position of something (*a bearing of 125 degrees*); to be clear about one's location (*to get one's bearings*); and the friction-reducing part of a machine (*it needs new bearings*). (See **berth**)

**Baroque** and **rococo** are both wielded by writers to mean elaborately detailed. Baroque was an artistic style that arose in Europe around the start of the seventeeth century, most obviously in painting, sculpture, architecture, design and music. In art its highly ornamented style aimed to produce drama and grandeur and its subjects were often religious. The work of Caravaggio and the music of Vivaldi have been cited as baroque. In its casual sense, it is used to suggest creations of great detail and extravagant style. Rococo followed baroque in the eighteenth century and, while still ornate, is generally regarded as lighter, more playful, fluid in line and more elegant in style. In its casual sense the word is taken to mean excessively ornate or intricate, particularly in music and literature.

A **baton** [bat-on] is a light, shaped piece of wood used by orchestra conductors, marching band leaders and relay runners; or a police officer's truncheon, which is heavier. A **batten** [bat-ən] is a strip of timber used in construction or joinery. To batten is to fasten hatches on a ship, or to fasten with battens (to batten down the hatches means to secure the hatches of a boat etc. ahead of bad weather, or to prepare for a crisis).

A **bazaar** [ba-zah] is a marketplace, especially in the Middle East; or a fund-raising sale at a fair etc. If something's **bizarre** [bi-zah] it's very strange.

A **beau** — rhymes with toe — is an ostentatious or old-fashioned term for a boyfriend. A **bough** — rhymes with how — is a branch of a tree. A **bow** — rhymes with how — is a bend at the head or waist in greeting, in response to applause etc., or to do so. You can bow to pressure, to weight or force (*a tree bowing to the wind*) or age (*bowed spine*). It's also the front of a ship. A **bow** — rhymes with toe — is a curved bend, a simple type of looped knot, an archer's weapon and an implement used to play stringed instruments such as a violin.

To be **bellicose** is to be aggressive and ready to fight (*a bellicose speech*), warlike. To be **belligerent** is to be aggressive and ready to argue (*a belligerent drunk*); or already fighting a war (*belligerent nations*).

**Below** is used to describe temperature, the position of objects on a flat plane, downstream or south of, and under real or figurative levels (*below the poverty line*). **Beneath** is slightly more formal, often used in context of being covered — blankets, water, earth — in a lower place, hiding (e.g. real personality or emotions), unworthy (*beneath contempt*). **Under** means less than, lower than. It's the most often used preposition, especially in phrases (*under consideration*), when talking about layers, beneath solid objects. **Underneath** is directly below, concealed by something; the underside of something.

**Beneficent** is doing good or resulting in good, charitable, generous (*a beneficent government*). **Munificent** is extremely generous of a giver or gift, lavish (*munificent sponsors*).

Something that's **benign** is gentle and kind or not harmful, especially as of a tumour. Something that's **malignant** is evil or intending ill; is harmful and threatening to life, especially as of a tumour. (See **baleful**, **malicious**)

A **bequest** is the act of giving by way of a will, or that which is given away. You **bequeath** your worldly goods. An **inquest** is a legal investigation, especially by a coroner into a death. A **request** is to ask for or demand, or the act of asking for something.

A **berth** is a place to sleep, especially on a train or ship; or a space for a vessel to manoeuvre or dock. To give something a wide berth means to avoid. A **birth** is the act of bearing young, or a beginning or commencement (*the birth of something amazing*). By extension, a woman can now birth a child, and Silicon Valley can birth an entire new way of doing business. (See **bare**)

When comparing two things that are good, **better** should be used for the more favoured item, and **best** for the item most favoured out of three or more things. The phrase 'best of both worlds' should be considered an oddity. Similarly, when comparing quality or harm or seriousness: if something has gone wrong, write 'Things took a turn for the **worse**', rather than **worst**. (See **former, latter**)

It is a mistake to write or say, as some have begun to, that someone who has preconceived ideas about someone or something is **bias** instead of biased, or **prejudice** when they mean prejudiced. Another in this vein is **jaundice** when the writer means jaundiced. Someone who is jaundiced is either suffering a medical condition in which the skin or whites of the eyes go yellow, or is bitterly resentful or cynical.

Four words that are sometimes confused, especially in the heat of an argument, are blatant, brazen and flagrant (and so sometimes fragrant). **Blatant** means done openly, especially in a crass manner; or is loud and noisy. A **brazen** act is one marked by shameless or contemptuous boldness. The word originally meant 'made of or like brass'; a once-common expression was 'bold as brass'. **Flagrant** means conspicuously bad or offensive, so a flagrant breach of the rules is severely frowned upon. A **fragrant** breach, if such a thing were possible, might be a robbery at a florist.

A **bloc** is a grouping of nations etc. for common purpose. Otherwise, for a mass of stone or wood, or to prevent, it's **block**.

If you are **bluff** you are goodheartedly blunt or direct. A bluff is a headland or cliff with a steep face, and to bluff means to mislead or deceive, especially with an unwarranted show of confidence. **Buff** means physically attractive, especially of a muscular nature, a term usually applied to men. It's also a brownish-yellow colour, a type of soft leather, and an enthusiast of a certain subject (*film buff*). As a verb it means to polish or shine. (Because buff also means unclothed skin, 'in the buff' means naked.)

To be **born** is to have been given birth to (*a child was born*), or having something from birth (*he's a born star*). **Borne** is a past participle of to bear or carry, as of a child or a hardship (*she has borne seven children*; *he had borne the cost*; *waterborne diseases*). (See **bare**, **birth**)

To **borrow** is to obtain temporarily (*May I borrow your pen?*). To **lend** is to allow someone the use of temporarily (*I'll lend the pen to you*) or to impart (*it lends the house a certain charm*). A **loan** is a temporary use of something, money lent; to loan is to lend (though it never means to impart).

Still very common is the misuse of **bought** and **brought**. Bought means purchased, being the past tense of buy (*they bought the house*). Brought means to have taken or carried, being the past tense of bring (*she brought her friend for company*). 'I bought it with me' is a common mistake. Perhaps confusing matters further is the phrasal verb 'to buy in', which means to purchase shares of something; to agree with an idea or plan; or to purchase something specially, as for an occasion (*we bought in extra flavours of ice-cream for the party*).

A **brake** is mechanical device to inhibit motion, as of a vehicle, or to reduce the speed of something with such a device. To **break** is to separate into pieces or the act or occurrence of breaking. It's also pause or interval, or sudden change.

**Brinkmanship** is the art or practice, especially in politics, of pushing a dangerous situation or confrontation to the limits of what is safe to get what you want. **One-upmanship** is the art or practice of staying one step ahead of another person or at least achieving a sense of superiority. The verb is one-upping.

To **broach** means most commonly to bring up a topic for discussion. It also means to pierce something to draw off liquid, to tip a boat on its side dangerously close to the waves, and to shape a hole with a tool, or such a tool. A **brooch** is an ornament worn high on the body, usually attached with a pin and clasp.

**Bygone** is a literary term for past, former (*bygone days*). In the plural it means past occurrences or grievances — 'Let bygones be bygones' means it's time to forget problems of the past and move on. **Foregone** means previous, past, completed. It's the past participle of 'forego', meaning to precede. A foregone conclusion is something so obvious that its occurrence is a near-certainty. (See **forgo**)

# C

A **cache** [kash or kaish] is a hidden collection of things or their hiding place (*a cache of weapons*); or temporary computer memory. **Cachet** [kash-ay] is something that gives a person or thing admiration, respect, prestige.

If someone is called **callous** they are thought unsympathetic, insensitive, indifferent, hard-hearted. A **callus** is an area of thickened and hardened skin, especially on the hands and feet. (See **loath, mucous**)

Words determining permission and possibility can trip up even careful users of the language. **Can** suggests a general truth or a solid possibility. (*It can be hard finding the perfect ride-on mover. There can be little doubt she's the right candidate. We can do this.*) **Could, might** or **may** suggest lesser possibility in such sentences. If making a request, use can or **could** (*can/could we please have some silence*). 'I can do that' means there is a good possibility. 'I could do that' means it's less likely. Use of could suggests conditions or other possibilities. If it's in the future the likelihood is higher. 'I could do that tomorrow' means there's a reasonable possibility. If you are asking permission to do something, **may** is regarded as the most formal, followed by could and then can. (*May I go out? Could I see you for a second? Can I take your hand?* The answer regarded as most polite, if stuffy, to all is: *You may.*) Formal requests or suggestions use might: 'Might you come?' 'Guests might be best to park on the far side of the venue.' May and can invite potential confusion. 'He may come to the party' can mean either that he has permission or that it is possible he will attend. To avoid confusion, most people will say 'He can come to the party' for permission and 'He may come to the party' if someone's wondering about catering numbers. May and **might** are interchangeable in many situations in the present. 'I may show up at the party' is much the same as 'I might show up at the party' though some sources suggest the latter indicates it's less likely. If you are speaking the day after the party, say 'He said he might show up'. 'He may have shown up' means the host didn't know if he was there, whereas 'He might have shown up' means he didn't and the speaker is either complaining or knew that he would have been there if things had gone differently. 'If she'd have studied harder, she might have got into university' is right, but 'The asteroid may have brought about the end of civilisation' is wrong and should instead be might, because we know it passed by harmlessly. Might is preferred if a future possibility is hypothetical or involves conditions: 'I might go to university if I get the grades/the asteroid doesn't hit.' If you're writing in reported speech that someone said they 'may', write that they 'might' — '"I may find the time," said Sue' will be 'Sue said she might find the time'.

**Cantankerous** means quarrelsome or contrary. **Rancorous** means coming from or marked by deep-seated resentment, i.e. rancour.

A **canvas** is a large piece of strong, closely woven cloth, often used to make sails and tents. It's also a piece of material for artists to paint on or a painting done on such material, or the floor of a boxing ring. To **canvass** is to solicit votes or seek support, to question, or to propose for discussion. (See **palate**)

The **capital** city of a country or state is where its government is situated. Capital also relates to the most important place for an activity (*the business capital*), a serious crime for which the justice system determines warrants execution (*capital punishment*), the upper-case form of letters, such as ABC (*capital letter*), the money or other assets of a household or business available for investment etc. (*capital expenditure*), a valuable resource (*political capital*), the collective power in society of those with money (*labour v capital*) and to mean leading or prominent (*of capital importance*) or, now dated, excellent (*a capital idea*). The broader head of a column is also called its capital. **Capitol** has a much narrower use. The capitol of a US state is a building or set of buildings where its state legislature meets. Capitol Hill refers to where the US Congress meets in America's capital, Washington DC.

To **career** means to move at high speed in an uncontrolled manner (*the car careered off the road*), the sense coming from an old French word for a racecourse — so any course, as with one's professional life. To **careen** means to lurch or tilt over, the sense — *carina* is Latin for keel — coming from the original of tilting a vessel for cleaning or while in the water. It is now also used in many parts of the world to mean moving at high speed in an uncontrolled manner, apparently influenced by career. This use upsets many traditionalists, but there is zero chance of a return to a clean divide outside of the nautical life.

A **carrot** remains a flavoursome root vegetable generally coloured orange, delivering vitamins A, K and B6 among other benefits, as well as being a metaphorically pleasant incentive in contrast to the punishment of the stick. A **carat** is a measure of the purity of gold (24 carat = pure) and a unit of weight for precious stones (1 carat = 200 mg). **Karat** is often used in North America for gold, with the abbreviation K. A **caret**, meanwhile, is the symbol ^ to indicate where a word or letter, for example, is to be inserted into text.

**Casuistry** is the determination of moral questions using case-based reasoning; or the use of clever but flawed arguments to persuade. **Sophistry** is the use of plausible but deceptive arguments to persuade. **Rhetoric** is the art or technique of speaking or writing well to persuade; or insincere language intended to manipulate. A rhetorical question is one asked for effect rather than with the expectation of an answer. (See **expedient**)

The word **caustic** means burning, corrosive, able to destroy living tissue; or severely critical or sarcastic. **Costive** has nothing to do with prices but means constipated (*a costive patient*), slow, reluctant, unforthcoming or ungenerous (*the most costive of writers*). (See **restive, sarcastic**)

The original meaning of **celibate** was unmarried, especially in accordance with a religious vow. But it is used now to mean both abstaining from sex (*she was single and celibate*) and unmarried (*celibate nuns and priests*). But **celibacy** in regards to religious orders is likely to indicate a person remains unmarried. **Chastity** is the state or practice of refraining from sex outside of marriage or entirely, though **chaste** behaviour may simply be decent or modest.

**Cellulite** is fat under the skin that causes a dimpling effect, typically used in relation to women's bodies. **Celluloid** is a plastic substance, but also figuratively cinema. **Cellulose** is a carbohydrate that forms the cell walls of most plants.

A **censor** is an official who grades publications or art works for public consumption (i.e. censors it) but to censor is also to prevent the public from seeing a work or works. **Censorious** means tending to find fault. To **censure** is to severely criticise, or harsh criticism. To **tonsure** is to shave the top of one's head as a rite of admission in some Christian orders. A tonsure is a hairstyle in this style, or a bald patch that resembles such a cut.

Except in punning headlines, don't confuse **cereal** — grain used for food, often breakfast eaten with milk — for **serial**. That means of a series, following the same pattern of behaviour (*a serial killer*), processed in order rather than parallel, a broadcast or print story in regular instalments, or a periodical publication.

**Chagrin** is annoyance or disappointment usually resulting from failure or humiliation. It can be used in a verbal sense: to chagrin is to annoy by disappointing or embarrassing. The word came from French, apparently with the sense of 'rough skin' and hence agitating situations. It is pronounced shag-rin or shə-grin; there is no need to attempt to say it as the French do. The related **shagreen** is a type of rough untanned leather or sharkskin used as an abrasive.

To be **chary** is to be cautious, wary, unwilling to take action. To be **leery** is wary, suspicious, distrustful. To **leer** is to look in a lascivious, sly or malicious way, or such a look. To be **wary** is to be cautious, on guard, watchful.

There are many -isms in English devoted to beliefs or attitudes. **Chauvinism** is, properly speaking, excessive and often unreasonable belief in the superiority of one's gender, country or kind. But most commonly now it is shorthand for male chauvinism, the belief that males are the superior of the species and do everything better. The word comes from a nationalistic French soldier devoted to the ideology of

Napoleon Bonaparte. In its original form it is close to **jingoism**, an extreme belief in the superiority of one's country, especially in regards to foreign policy. **Patriotism** is devotion, often unquestioningly, to one's country. **Parochialism** is a local, narrow or similarly restricted outlook. The other side of the 'specific doctrine, cause or theory' of many -isms is that of patronage. **Favouritism** is an inclination to partiality. **Cronyism** is the use or employment by a person of power of their friends, with no regard for their qualifications. **Nativism** is the policy of favouring the interests of native inhabitants of a country over immigrants. **Nepotism**, from Italian and French words relating to nephew, is giving jobs and favours to relatives.

**Checkmate** is the winning chess move involving the king or to put your opponent into checkmate. Figuratively, it's also a defeat or situation that has no escape, or to defeat someone in such a way. That definition is close to **deadlock**: the point in a discussion or conflict in which neither party is willing to compromise and no progress can be made; or means to cause such a position. An **impasse**, likewise, is a negotiation in which no progress can be made. A **Mexican standoff** is a situation or confrontation, usually of three or more parties, in which none will emerge the winner. Not surprisingly, it's often depicted as three men with large hats and guns pointed at each other. A **stalemate** is a situation in which further action or progress between opposing parties seems unlikely. You can stalemate someone. It comes from chess again, being a drawn position in which a player is not checkmated but can only move into check.

If you're confused when it comes to describing things that are a bit fake or obvious, you aren't alone: there's plenty of semantic overlap. A **cheesy** movie is one that is obviously inauthentic, unsubtle or trying too hard but can still be enjoyed. A **corny** one is trite, old-fashioned or tiresomely sentimental. A **hammy** one is marked by unnatural, exaggerated and often self-conscious theatricality. Something **hokey**, often a performance rather than a whole film, say, is overdone, exaggeratedly sentimental or obviously contrived. If it's **mawkish**, it's insipid or overly or falsely sentimental. If it's **schlocky**, as of a movie or TV show, it's of inferior quality or value. If it's **schmaltzy**, on the other hand (from the Yiddish for chicken fat), it's excessively sentimental, florid, showy. And if it's **ropey**, it's inferior or unbelievable, not a good example of its kind.

Another crowd of words that are sometimes interchanged involve aesthetic taste. **Chintzy** means cheap and often poor quality. **Glitzy** denotes shiny or show-off. **Kitschy** means having vulgar bad taste, garish or sentimental, and is often said of art or décor. **Ritzy** is almost the opposite, being luxuriously elegant, apparently after the Ritz hotel chain, though there is a slightly judgmental whiff of 'fanciness'. **Ditzy**, usually said of people, typically women, is scatterbrained. **Klutzy**, from Yiddish, means clumsy, as of a klutz, a clumsy or stupid person.

There was a time when we thought four humours decided human personality, influenced by four bodily organs and four bodily fluids. All liquids in the body were derived from these four. If you were more of a **choleric** temperament you were ruled by yellow bile/choler (spleen), so hot tempered, irritable and ambitious (**splenetic** — full of **spleen** — and **bilious**, or full of **bile**, both meaning bad tempered or irritable, and **gall**, meaning impudence, come from this idea). If you were **melancholic**, black bile was your fluid (from the gall bladder) and you were gloomy, quiet and serious. The **phlegmatic** type, ruled by phlegm (brain/lungs), was not easily excited, stolidly calm. And **sanguine** folk, ruled by blood (liver), were optimistic and confident. The usage still describes emotional states, even if the categorisation now intellectually sits alongside astrology. (See **jovial**, **stoic**)

It's hardly surprising that chord and cord are sometimes used mistakenly, given that their etymologies interweave and a spelling change was made in the eighteenth century to reduce confusion. A **chord**, apart from having specific mathematical, aeronautical and architectural meanings, is a group of musical notes sounded together. To strike/touch a chord is to engender sympathy; to strike the right chord is to successfully achieve an appropriate response in others. A **cord** is a thin, flexible line of rope, string or wire of twisted strands; or a type of ribbed fabric, usually corduroy. It's also used to refer to parts of the anatomy that resemble a length of cord, particularly the spinal cord, vocal cords or umbilical cord. Vocal cords in particular are often spelled as vocal chords, probably because of the sound association, but this is regarded as non-standard usage. To cut the (umbilical) cord of someone is to stop supporting them, especially financially or emotionally; if someone cuts the cord themselves they set out on their own, especially creatively.

A **cinch** [sinch] is something easy (*this test is a cinch*); as a verb it means to tighten like a belt. A **cliché** [klee-shay] is a hackneyed expression. A **clinch** is an embrace, especially a loving one, or conversely a close-in scuffle or boxing hold. You can clinch — win — an argument or a deal, clinch a nail by beating it down sideways once it has entered a piece of wood, or a length of rope on a boat using a particular knot. A clincher is something decisive in an argument or a deal.

The term **cis**, short for cisgender, is increasingly used, particularly in discussions of sexual identities and social justice, to describe someone who feels that they are the same gender as the physical body they were born with, as in cis-female, as compared to transgender (often simply trans). The word-element comes from the Latin preposition cis meaning 'on this side' in a physical sense, such as cismontane or cisalpine, from the Latin for 'on this [the Roman] side of the Alps', as compared to ultramontane or transmontane. In English, cis also took on a time sense, in terms as cis-Elizabethan; in chemistry concerning molecules with the same formula but arranged differently; and in the 21st century in gender identity. (See **gender**, **LGBT**)

To **cite** is to quote as evidence, especially in scholarly texts (*the author's work was cited*); to mention (*speed is often cited as a cause of car accidents*); to formally commend or praise (*she was cited for her courage in the field*); or to call to appear before a court (*the company was cited for four breaches of the Fair Trading Act*). The noun is citation. **Sight** is the ability to see, or a vision or panorama. A **site** is a place or location, especially for a forthcoming building, short for website; to site is to position something.

A **claque** is a group of sycophantic supporters, or a group of paid applauders. A member of these groups is a claqueur. A **clique** is an exclusive group of people who don't readily admit newcomers. Such a group might be termed cliquey or cliquish.

A **classic** is that which is judged to be of quality or a superior or memorable example, or popular for a long period of time (*this song is a classic*; *that football game was a classic*). It's something that's typical (*a classic example of 1970s architecture*) or excellent and timeless (*a classic album*). Particularly of clothing, it's stylish and not particularly affected by fashion trends (*a classic three-piece suit from Gieves & Hawkes*). **Classical** means relating to Roman and Greek antiquity; classical art forms are those, particularly music, adhering to longstanding formal traditions. In academia, the **classics** are the works of ancient Greek and Latin writers and thinkers. More broadly, they are famous or well regarded literature of the past, such as Shakespeare, Tolstoy, Jane Austen. (See **economic**, **historic**)

**Climactic** is to do with a climax or climaxes (*a climactic finish*). **Climatic** is to do with the climate (*climatic changes*). **Climacteric** means of critical importance (*a climacteric phase of the campaign*). A climacteric is any critical time (*a climacteric in history*) or a critical time in a human life, such as menopause or andropause, when major change occurs. A climacteric phase happens in some fruits when growth is finished and rapid ripening occurs.

**Coarse** is rough, uncouth, vulgar; not elegant, inferior; not fine, as in grains. A **course** is a path, channel, method, way, procedure. It's a series of lectures or of medical treatments or drugs, an area for golf etc. or one part of a meal. It also means to flow (*the tears coursed down her red cheeks*).

**Cogent** means forcefully convincing or persuasive, appealing strongly to the power of reason, based on evidence. **Coherent** means capable of logical and understandable speech or thought; logical, consistent and orderly; having the quality of sticking together. (See **incoherent**)

**Cognisant**, also cognizant, means having awareness or knowledge of (*cognisant of the facts*), taking official note of, especially in a legal context, and mindful (*be cognisant of danger*). Cognisant is sometimes mistaken for meaning having conscious awareness, as of a woozy hospital patient. The **cognoscenti** are people who are particularly well informed about a subject (*arts cognoscenti*); the singular is cognoscente.

A **colloquy** is a formal or serious conversation, a written dialogue or a gathering for discussion of religious questions. **Colloquial** means related to informal or conversational use of language. An **obloquy** is abusive or critical language about someone; or disgrace or loss of reputation. A **soliloquy** is a long speech to oneself that reveals one's thoughts or feelings, the speaker being oblivious to whether she or he is being heard, most commonly seen in theatre.

The difference between a **coma** and a **persistent vegetative state** (PVS) is that while both lack conscious awareness of their surroundings, those in a coma do not appear to have a sleep–wake cycle but PVS patients do. Patients in a persistent vegetative state might move, open and close their eyes, react to stimuli or make noises; coma patients do not.

**Comity** is a friendly, civil or courteous state between people, nations or organisations, the mutual recognition of customs and laws between nations, or such a group of countries (*comity of nations*); less formally, it is a friendly, considerate atmosphere. (See **polity**)

To be **complacent** is to be self-satisfied to the point of smugness and reluctance to change. To be **complaisant** is to be eager to please or condone without protest (*complaisant journalists*). **Compliant** is obedient, submissive (*a compliant workforce*); or complying with regulations etc. (*a compliant café*).

To **complement** is to add features or variety to; a complement is something that completes or combines to make a whole. To **compliment** is to praise or flatter; a compliment is an expression of praise or flattery. That which is **complementary** completes or makes up a whole. If it's **complimentary** it is either free as part of service or it offers praise.

**Complex** and **complicated** are often interchanged, most of the time without confusion. A complex system is one that has many interconnected parts but has been built or formed this way to deal with its task and likely future tasks. Complexity is intrinsic. A complicated system — or problem — can also have many interconnected parts but has probably been made complicated because of external factors. It is one that would be difficult to understand or describe — and presumably fix. You are more likely to make a system or situation more complicated than more complex. In other meanings, a complex is a collection of buildings on one site, a closely linked grouping or system of things or, in psychology, a group of repressed thoughts and feelings that can influence personality or behaviour. (See **simple**)

Two commonly misused words are **compose** and **comprise**. Compose means (when it doesn't mean to create, arrange or calm) to constitute or make up (the parts of); comprise means to include, consist of or make up (a whole). It might be helpful to think of comprise as referring to the whole, as in: the menagerie comprises two dogs, five cats and four birds. And compose as its parts: water is composed of hydrogen and oxygen molecules. The passive construction 'is comprised of' is increasingly accepted but don't write or say 'it comprises of'.

To be **condescending** is to show a superior attitude towards someone or something. To be **sanctimonious** is to make a show of being morally superior to others, or feign moral correctness or dutifulness, especially hypocritically. To be **self-righteous** is to have or show smug confidence in one's own moral correctness while judging others' to be wrong. If you are simply **righteous** you are morally correct; if you are **self-regarding** you are self-centred, considering yourself and your own interests most important. If you are **supercilious** you behave arrogantly superior to others, showing contemptuous indifference. (See **patronise**)

A **confidant** is someone you confide in. To be **confident** is to have confidence.

To **conspire** is to plot with others. To **expire** is to come to an end, especially of a period of valid use, to cease living, or to breathe out. To **inspire** is to arouse people to action or confidence, through emotional response or by example, bring about (*the book inspired a thousand imitations*), or to breathe in. To **perspire** is to sweat. To **transpire** is to give off water, or to happen (*it transpired that the deal was off*).

A **consul** is a state official in a foreign country who guards a nation's citizens and interests. A **council** is an administrative body of people, most often formally constituted and meeting regularly. **Counsel** is formal or professional advice, or a legal adviser conducting a defence. To counsel is to advise, especially in a formal or professional way.

**Contemporary** is used to mean both occurring or belonging to the same time (*contemporary accounts of the battle*) and belonging to the present, modern-day (*contemporary painting*).

If something is **contemptible** it deserves contempt. If someone is **contemptuous** they are feeling, showing or expressing contempt.

**Continual** means that something continues with breaks. **Continuous** continues without breaks.

A **contusion** is a bruise. A **haematoma** (US: hematoma) is a collection of blood on the surface of the skin outside blood vessels.

A **conundrum** is a difficult or insoluble problem or, traditionally, a riddle that may be answered by a pun. A **dichotomy** is a problem in which there is a clear difference between two things, or a division into contrasting groups. A **dilemma** is a choice between two undesirable options; it is widely used to mean any difficult decision or situation, though language guides still advise against that. An **enigma** is something that is mysterious or that has a hidden meaning, such as a puzzle or riddle. A **paradox** is a statement that seems to be contradictory or opposed to common sense but which may still be true; or a person or thing having qualities that appear to be in direct opposition. A **quandary** is a state of uncertainty or confusion.

To **cow** is to intimidate someone so as to cause them to submit to one's wishes (*they were cowed into not speaking*). To **cower** is to recoil or reduce oneself in height, or squat in fear. To **kowtow** is to act in a completely subservient and usually obsequious fashion, or to kneel and touch the forehead to the ground in the traditional Chinese custom. A kowtow is such an act of submission.

Despite their appearance, **crapulence** and its adjectives **crapulent** and **crapulous** have nothing to do with excrement or poor quality, despite what you might read in some places (or see: *The Simpsons*). They seem to be misused as synonyms for general crappiness or mentally wallowing in an unhealthy environment, such as immorality or lowbrow television habits. They are literary words for drunkenness and drunken behaviour, coming directly from a Latin word for very drunk. An older meaning is also given of illness or indisposition resulting from excessive drinking or eating.

To **creak** is to make a long, varying high noise, like an old door, or such a noise. A **creek** is a small stream.

A **credible** witness is believable, convincing or trustworthy. To be **creditable** is to be worthy of praise, though not high praise. To be **credulous** is to be gullible. (See **incredible**)

Strictly speaking, a **crescendo** [crə-shen-doh] is a gradual increase in loudness in a piece of music, or a passage of music in which this happens. A piece of music or sound, such as drumming, can crescendo; and a crescendo beat is one that rises in loudness. But another meaning has evolved from the loudest point of a gradual increase in sound: that of the peak in noise (or activity or intensity) itself. Many people will say 'The noise in the room rose to a crescendo' or 'The level of criticism had reached a crescendo by the end of the week'. It's such a useful metaphor that there is no chance of it returning to its technical bounds.

The **crotch** is the gap between the legs or the matching part of trousers. A **crutch** is a stick with a horizontal part for support under the arm for someone who is injured or disabled, or a metaphorical something on which someone depends for help or support, usually too much.

**Crypto** means secret, hidden, concealed, not publicly admitted (cryptography is the study of secret codes, while a crypto-fascist keeps hidden their support of fascism). **Pseudo** means having the appearance of, but not actually being, sham, false, wannabe (*pseudo-intellectual*). In chemical compounds, it means bearing a close resemblance to (*pseudoephedrine*). **Quasi** means resembling but not being, almost but not quite, virtual (*quasi-scientific*). (See **poetaster**)

A **cue** is a signal or prompt for action, stimulus, reminder, suggestion. And it's a stick with a felt end for table ball games. As a verb it means to signal, prompt or insert into a sequence. A **queue** is a line of people, vehicles, computer commands. As a verb it means to line up in a row.

**Cunctation** is an unusual, suggestive word for the action of delaying a decision. Synonyms are delay, procrastination, hesitation. (See **equivocation**)

To **curb** is to restrain or check; in the US, it's the border between the road and the sidewalk or footpath. In the UK and elsewhere, the **kerb** is the border between the road and footpath.

A **cymbal** is a percussion instrument made of brass. A **symbol** is a representational sign.

**Cynicism** is a disposition, attitude or act of general distrust in others' motives. **Scepticism** is an attitude or disposition of doubt without proof, or the philosophical theory that certain knowledge is uncertain or impossible.

A **cynosure** [si-ni-zure] is something that is a centre of attention (*the cynosure of all critics*). A **sinecure** [sigh-ni-cure] is a paid job or role that requires little or no work.

# D

**Damp** is moisture or humidity, but to damp down is to reduce the intensity of something, such as a fire, an emotion etc. (*damping down the economy*). You can damp the sound of a musical instrument by lessening the vibration of its strings. A building can have shock absorbers to damp — lessen — the shaking of an earthquake. To **dampen** is to make wet, but to dampen down is to make something weaker, such as anger, enthusiasm, spirit, demand. To **tamp** down is to pack material into a hole or container, such as earth, tobacco, coffee.

**Debris** is the remains of something after it has been broken or destroyed; it's rubble, wreckage, ruins. In medical contexts, it's waste in the form of fragments or particles. **Detritus** is waste or rubbish after an event, erosion or organic decomposition. (See **flotsam**)

**Decent** [DEE-sənt] means pleasant and obliging (*a decent sort*), or respectable. A **descent** [dəh-SENT] is the action or process of going downward, descending; or one's ancestral lineage (*of Scottish descent*).

The word **decimate**, which dates from Roman times, originally meant to kill one in ten soldiers as punishment for serious disobedience. For centuries it has been used more widely to mean removing or killing a significant proportion of something, causing great destruction or harm to, or greatly reducing the strength of something (*a virus decimated beehives in the region*; *jobs were decimated by automation*; *the bus service was decimated by budget cuts*). Some traditionalists insist it should only be used in its original sense, but the fact that we no longer slaughter every tenth mutinous soldier no doubt helped the change in meaning, and it must be time to celebrate the fact and move on.

To **declaim** is to speak dramatically or rhetorically (*she declaimed her take on the matter*) or to protest or speak against something (*the priest declaimed sin in society*). To **disclaim** is to deny or renounce claim to or responsibility for (*she disclaimed knowing the accused*). To **proclaim** is to announce officially or publicly (*I proclaim them the best band ever*). (See **casuistry**)

To **defer** is to put off until later or to give way to someone else (*I defer to your authority*). To **demur** is to show reluctance or voice opposition, or to delay or hesitate (*he demurred on the subject*). **Demure** is modest and reserved in manner, often affectedly so. To **deter** is to turn away or try to prevent (*she deterred his entry*).

To **defuse** [dee-fyooz] is to disarm, make less dangerous or tense (*defuse the explosive device*; *defuse a situation*). To **diffuse** [di-fyooz] is to spread over a large area. Something that's diffuse [di-fyoos] is spread or not concentrated (*diffuse communities*; *diffuse light*). You can defuse tension but not diffuse it; you can diffuse technology but not necessarily defuse its impact.

If you indulge in **deification** you are worshipping, making a god out of something or someone or raising them to the status of a god. The verb is to **deify**. **Reification** is making something intangible real or concrete; the verb is **reify**. **Ideation** is a formal word often used in psychological contexts concerning forming ideas (*suicidal ideation*); the verb is **ideate**. **Edification** means personal improvement, especially of a moral, spiritual or intellectual nature; the verb is **edify**. **Efficacious**, sometimes used in similar contexts, means effective, capable of producing the desired result.

A few serious critical words resemble each other, and can be confused. If something is **deleterious** it is dangerous or harmful (*deleterious effects*). If a person is dubbed **sententious**, they are given to moralising in an affected manner (*sententious dialogue*) or are in the practice of expressing maxims or aphorisms. If something is **tendentious** it's biased or partisan.

To **delude** is to mislead, deceive (*deluding the public*). To **preclude** is to deliberately leave out or to make impossible (*preclude the chance*).

A **delusion** is a hallucination or an irrational or false belief, often as a symptom of mental disorder. An **illusion** is an incorrect perception (*an optical illusion*) or impression (*an illusion of happiness*); or the state of being deceived or an example of such. An **allusion** is an indirect reference. (See **allusive**, **delude**)

A **démarche** [day-marsh] is a diplomatic or political step or manoeuvre. **Détente** [day-tont] is a lessening of tensions, especially between countries, often by way of agreements or negotiations. **Entente cordiale** [on-tont-cordee-ahl] is friendly understanding between political powers. **Rapprochement** [rah-prosh-mont] is agreement or resumption of friendly relations between countries or factions.

**Demilitarisation** is reduction in size of a nation's military presence, often as a result of a peace agreement. **Demobilisation** is disbanding of troops, or moving from a war footing to one of less active service, often as a result of a victory.

**Denunciation** is public accusation or condemnation; the verb is to denounce. **Enunciation** is clear articulation of speech, or a formal declaration; the verb is to enunciate. **Pronunciation** is pattern of speech as moderated by stress, inflection, cadence, intonation etc. To pronounce also means to announce formally (*he was pronounced dead*) and to pass judgment upon (*pronounce a verdict*).

A **dependant** is someone who is reliant upon another. To be **dependent** is to be reliant upon another.

To **deplore** is to condemn (*I deplore capital punishment*). To **implore** is to plead or appeal for something, often from someone (*she implored him to stop*).

To **deprecate** is to express disapproval of something or someone (*excess is deprecated; self-deprecating humour*). In software, to be deprecated is to mark a feature for obsolescence in the next upgrade. Deprecate is increasingly used to mean belittle (*a deprecated artist*) or play down (*deprecate his talents*) but traditionalists argue that **depreciate** should be used in this context. To depreciate is to lessen the value of something over a period of time — depreciation — and hence belittle or undervalue (*depreciating his record*), but the crossover in usage seems well established.

**Depredation** is to plunder; the verb is to depredate. **Deprivation** is the act of depriving someone of something they need or want.

To be **derisive** is to be mocking, scornful (*a derisive laugh*). To be **derisory** is to be laughable or deserving of scorn, particularly ridiculously small (*a derisory pay offer*).

A **descendant** is one who descends from — so is related to, and is often confused with — an **ancestor** or **forebear**, both typically more than a couple of generations removed. To be **descendent** is a less common word meaning descending from an ancestor, or downward-moving.

A **desert** [dez-it] is a region with sparse or no vegetation, usually because of low rainfall. To **desert** [de-zert] is to abandon. Just deserts — not desserts — means to get what you deserve, especially a punishment. **Dessert** [de-zert] is a late, often sweet course of a meal.

**Determinately** is having precise limits. **Determinedly** means with determination. **Deterministically** comes from determinism, the idea that every event, including human action, has a cause that is outside of human will.

**Depilation** is the removal of bodily hair. **Dilapidation** is the state of being rundown, partially ruined.

A **diagnosis** is the identification of the nature of an illness or problem. A **prognosis** is a forecast or the likely course of a medical or other problem.

To **die** is to cease to be, whether person, animal or plant, or non-living things to expire or stop working. A die is a metal-shaping tool. Dice is almost universal as both singular and plural of the multi-sided cube used in games. The singular — die — is rarely heard outside the cliché 'The die is cast', meaning there's no going back now. To **dye** is to colour fabric. A dyed-in-the-wool fan is one who doesn't vary and doesn't compromise in their devotion.

The subject of contrasting difference can raise voices or hackles. '**Different from**' is probably the most commonly used version in both the UK and US, both in written and spoken language, and some traditionalists refuse to accept any other view. Yet both '**different to**' and '**different than**' have been deployed for centuries by brilliant writers and language authorities. Supporters say something differs from something else so how can it be different to? Others note 'indifferent to' as a useful guide. 'Different than' is used more frequently in the US than the UK, and 'different to' is rarer in the US, but it doesn't make either wrong, unless they introduce ambiguity. Context can play a role. 'Different than' might be a step too far for followers of UK form unless they are trying to insert an American flavour into their writing, but it has been suggested it is best used before a clause: 'The syllabus is now much different than I remember.' But: 'The syllabus is very different to how I remember it.' And: 'The syllabus is now very different from that of a decade ago.' Even though it's largely a preference, because many publication style guides will prescribe 'different from', it may be useful to defer.

A **dilettante** is a dabbler, one who takes up an art or activity in a superficial or uncommitted way. Allied is a **flibbertigibbet**, a flighty, frivolous person who probably talks too much. They are flibberty-gibberty, an imitation of rapid speech. A **debutante** is a young woman being formally presented to others deemed to be of a high social rank, usually through a series of events.

**Discomfit** and **discomfort** are not related etymologically, but as verbs they now share a sense of making someone uneasy or embarrassed (*he was discomfited by the attention*; *the truth discomforted me*). Discomfit also suggests frustrating or confusing, some sources say, while discomfort suggests pain (*discomforting symptoms*). Discomfort is often used as a noun, meaning slight pain (*abdominal discomfort*), concern (*discomfort and squirming embarrassment*) and that which makes someone uncomfortable (*discomforts of pregnancy*).

**Discreet** means judicious or unobtrusive (*discreet enquiries*). The noun is discretion. **Discrete** means distinct or separate (*discrete elements*). The noun is discreteness.

If someone is **disenchanted** they are disillusioned, or disappointed by something or someone previously held in high regard (*a disenchanted fan*). If they are **disenfranchised** they don't have the right to vote or have been deprived of that right. Or they feel deprived of an important right or privilege, or access to having one's view heard or the ability to change one's society (*poor and disenfranchised*).

**Disinformation** is false information often spread secretly that is intended to make people believe something is true, for example, government propaganda. **Misinformation** is false or incorrect information passed on either unintentionally or that's intended to deceive the recipient.

Someone who's **disingenuous** is not being entirely honest or suggesting frankness that's not real. A disingenuous offer is an insincere one. **Ingenious**, said of a person, means clever, inventive, novel in thought. Said of a device or idea, it means cleverly conceived or executed. **Ingenuity** generally applies to cleverly inventive people, but can be used for devices or inventive creation. **Ingenuous** is a less common word than disingenuous meaning innocent, unsuspecting, naively trusting. An **ingénue** [un-zhə-noo or un-zhay-nyu] is an unsophisticated or artless young woman, especially as portrayed in a film or play. (See **artful**)

**Disinterested** means impartial, dispassionate. Its use as a synonym for **uninterested** — meaning not interested or bored — is, though widely used, still generally regarded as incorrect. Prefer impartial or unbiased, or bored or indifferent. (See **fulsome**, **moot**, **nonplussed**)

To **dissemble** is to pretend, feign, disguise, conceal one's real feelings or beliefs (*dissembling politicians*; *she dissembled an enthusiasm*). To **dissimulate** is to hide one's true feelings or character (*he tried to dissimulate his identity*). To **simulate** is to pretend that something that is not the case is the case, or to mimic. To **stimulate** is to excite.

To **dissipate** means to spread something or to squander, but **dissipated** means overindulging in sensual pleasures (*dissipated behaviour*). **Dissolute** similarly means indulging in pleasurable activities (*a dissolute lifestyle*). (See **effete**)

**Distinct** means recognisably different or clearly separate (*two distinct types of tree*; *distinct communities*); able to be perceived clearly by the senses (*a distinct outline in the sky*); or, in emphasis, unmistakably clear (*a distinct possibility*). **Distinctive** means providing a difference that serves to distinguish, characteristic (*the distinctive flight of the pelican*).

A **diuretic** is a substance that encourages urination. An **emetic** encourages vomiting. A **laxative** encourages emptying of bowels. **Hepatic** relates to the liver. **Renal** relates to the kidneys.

To **divert** means to effect a change of course, to deflect, or to amuse. To **invert** is to flip, reverse or turn inwards. To **pervert** is to lead towards the illicit or abnormal. To **subvert** is to undermine or overthrow.

To be **docile** is to be easily managed or handled or taught, submissive. **Facile** means superficial, achieved with little effort or difficulty, or arrived at without the proper rigour or effort.

**Doctrinaire** means following or insistent on fixed beliefs or practices — that is, doctrines — without regard to their practicality. **Dogmatic** means relating to dogma — a system of beliefs, particularly religious or political, that are accepted without question or doubt. A dogmatic opinion is asserted as if authoritative and undeniable. A dogmatic person is prone to making such statements, or unwilling to consider other points of view.

Something that's **doubtful** is unlikely or raises sometimes serious doubts. If it's **dubious** it also causes doubts, but a dubious idea can be suspect or questionable (*dubious friends*; *of dubious value*).

**Dour** [doo-er or dow-er] means unhappy, unfriendly or severe, and is generally used to describe people's appearance or general manner. The first pronunciation often given rhymes it with 'cure' — the word probably comes from Latin *durus*, meaning hard, as in durable — but is now following spelling, particularly in the US, to more often rhyme with 'flour'.

To **douse** is to make wet, put out a fire or flame with liquid, or stop a light from shining by, for example, covering it. Broadly, it means to extinguish or severely reduce (*douse her enthusiasm*). To **dowse** is to attempt to find underground water, minerals or other unseen materials by using a divining rod or similar tool.

To **draft** is to draw up an outline or sketch, or in the US to conscript. A draft is a preliminary sketch or outline, a money order, US conscription or US big-league sports selection. A **draught** is a current of air, a serving of alcohol or the depth of water required to sink a ship. All US uses are spelled draft.

To **draw** is to produce an image, to pull or extract, to equal in a competition, to cause a golf ball to gently deviate from the handedness of the player, being the opposite of a fade. A draw is a selection by ballot, a score that's even or not completed, a golf shot or an inhalation on a cigarette. A **drawer** is either a sliding compartment in a desk or other furniture, or someone who draws.

**Dual** means having two parts or elements, often similar or complementary (*dual-purpose*). A **duel** is a controlled, prearranged fight between two people or any struggle between two people.

# E

Be clear if you mean unusual or free-thinking. **Eccentric** means odd or unconventional, especially personal behaviour (*he was charmingly eccentric*), from the idea of an astronomical body deviating from a circular path (*an eccentric orbit*). **Eclectic** means drawn from a wide and diverse range of sources (*eclectic taste*).

**Economic** is used in regards to economics or trade and usually suggests being profitable (*an economic solution*). **Economical** means thrifty, not wasteful, giving good value (*an economical car*). Being economical with the truth is to lie or deliberately withhold useful information. (See **classic**, **historic**)

**Effete** has a continuum of meaning including a coded insult. It is used to mean affected and ineffectual; marked by decadence, weakness or lost vitality; soft or delicate; effeminate; and, historically, no longer fertile (it comes from Latin *effetus*, i.e. worn out from childbearing). **Jejune**, originally meaning empty of food so intellectually barren, is now used to mean naive, unsophisticated, and (of ideas) dull, insipid.

For both of these vague and easily misunderstood terms, use one of those words instead. Of a plant, **etiolated** means pale and spindly, especially through lack of sunlight. Of a person it means pale and weak, and is applied to artistic or aristocratic types. To be called **fey** is to be whimsically unusual and vague, otherworldly, slightly crazy, or camp. **Camp** describes — of a person or artwork — ostentatiously theatrical or deliberately exaggerated, and is possibly derogatory of effeminate gay male behaviour.

The abbreviation **e.g.** is short for the Latin phrase *exempli gratia*, meaning that which might be more effectively substituted or 'for example'. It is used when an example is presented of what is being discussed. (*The animals went in two by two, e.g. camels and horses and zebras.*) The abbreviation **i.e.** is short for the Latin phrase *id est*, meaning 'that is'. It is used when an explanation or clarification of what is being discussed is needed: 'in other words'. (*I enjoy most spending time with my favourite person, i.e. myself.*) The abbreviation **viz**, which is less common than e.g. or i.e. and often written as viz., is short for the Latin phrase *videlicet*, meaning 'that is to say' or 'namely'; it differs from the other two in that it expands on what has been said rather than simply restating it, and what follows is generally a complete or near-complete list of what is meant rather than a selection of examples. (*He was convicted of several crimes, viz theft as a servant, fraud, embezzlement.*) Don't confuse viz with **vis-à-vis** [veez ah vee], a phrase borrowed from French — literally 'face to face' — which means 'with regard to' or 'in relation to'. (*There are serious gaps vis-à-vis security and personnel.*)

**Egregious** means flagrant or conspicuously bad (*an egregious breach of protocol*). It originally meant extremely good but does not any longer. **Grievous** means serious or flagrant, causing severe pain, grief or suffering (*grievous bodily harm*). Don't write or pronounce it gree-vee-us. (See **fulsome**)

If you use **either** with two singular alternatives it requires a singular verb, and should only apply to two alternatives (*You may borrow either the Murakami or the Reacher — either is fine.*) If one or the other of the alternatives is plural, the verb is plural. (*Either she or they are the problem.*) If pronouns are in use, the one closer to the verb governs person and number. (*Neither he nor you* have *any chance of passing now. Either they or she* is *fit for service.*) Either should apply to two alternatives; if there are more, use 'any' or 'any one' (*she could choose either of these two cars, or any one of those over there*). It was once considered incorrect to say 'There are seats on either side of the field' or 'It's not considered a win by either party' because either suggests a choice (for one or the other, or each), but no longer. **Neither** should similarly apply to only two alternatives. If there are more than two, use 'not any' or 'none'. It is regarded as good English style to use alternatives that are closely matched and elegantly balance the sentence, usually by placing the either/or and neither/nor close to the alternatives (*you can choose to go to either Victoria or Canterbury* rather than *you are either going to Victoria or Canterbury*).

To **eke** something out is to make it last longer by consuming or using frugally, often used in the phrase 'to eke out a living'. **Eek** is an exclamation, uttered semi-voluntarily and usually humorously, that expresses surprise or horror.

In geometry, an **ellipse** is an oval shape. An **ellipsis** is the omission of words from a written sentence or speech that are superfluous or able to be understood by context; it also refers to the set of three dots in text . . . indicating that a word or words have been left out. Difficulty sometimes arises because **elliptical** is used to mean either relating to an oval or to an ellipsis. If it's the first, it could mean an idea that loops back on itself. But it usually means, in relation to writing or speech, that which is extremely economical, and so perhaps difficult to understand. An **eclipse**, just to be clear, is the obscuring of one planet, moon or star by another; as a verb, it means to surpass and so put someone or something in one's shadow.

**Emancipated** is to be freed from someone else's power (*emancipated slaves*) or of social, political or legal restraint; or to be less inhibited by social or moral convention (*emancipated from expectations*). **Emasculated** is to be deprived of power, virility or strength, especially of a man by a woman (*he felt emasculated by her career*), originally meaning castrated. **Emaciated** is very thin, wasted (*he looked emaciated*).

To **embody** is to give bodily form to, or to include or represent into a cohesive whole. To **engender** is to bring into existence or give rise to, to propagate.

**Eminent** means prominent (*an eminent physician*). Expressions such as 'eminently publishable' of books are considered acceptable to mean notably. **Immanent** is a less common term meaning inherent, existing within, subjective (*immanent in law*), but is sometimes mistaken for **imminent**, meaning about to occur (*an imminent release*).

An **emission** is that which is emitted or given out. An **omission** is omitting or leaving something out. A **remission** is about reduction — of debt, in the length of a prison sentence, the forgiveness of sins, or a period of improved health for someone suffering an illness.

Two words that come from the same source but are not interchangeable are emotional and emotive. **Emotional** means relating to the emotions (*emotional problems*) or characterised by or expressing strong feelings (*an emotional performance*; *an emotional young man*). **Emotive** means arousing strong feelings (*an emotive issue*) or expressing one's feelings rather than being dispassionate (*he used emotive language to persuade the crowd*).

**Empathy** is the ability to experience and share the feelings of others even if they haven't been explicitly communicated (*deep empathy for prisoners*). An artwork can be regarded as having great empathy if the artist is successful in getting across what they wish to convey. **Sympathy** is common compassion for another's plight even if one has not experienced it (*sympathy letters*), or simply mutual affection or understanding (*conservative sympathies*).

That which is **endemic** is common or regularly found in a group of people, situation or activity (*poverty is endemic in this state of the US*); native to a region or locality (*endemic lizards*); or prevalent in a particular area (*endemic diseases*). An **epidemic** is an outbreak of an infectious disease that spreads widely in an area or population (*a flu epidemic*); sudden and rapid spread of an unwelcome phenomenon (*an epidemic of racist attacks*); or widely prevalent (*obesity is reaching epidemic proportions*). A **pandemic** is an outbreak of disease over an entire country or wider.

To **energise** is to give energy, rouse. The adjective is energising (*an energising talk*). To **enervate** is to deprive of force or energy, to weaken. The adjective is enervating (*an enervating physical battle*). The etymology is *ex* + *nervus* — literally, to cut the sinews out of.

Traditionalists frown on **enormity** being used as a synonym for enormousness — which it was influenced by — because it originally meant a departure from the norm in terms of moral or legal behaviour. That meaning of great size has solidified, but in formal use the word means the extreme size, seriousness or extent of something that can be judged as bad; an evil act or sin, or great wickedness; or the shocking scale or importance of something negative. Dictionaries do point out that even when being used in a newer sense it is usually applied to circumstances that deviate markedly from the norm, or relates to something of great difficulty (*the enormity of the crime; the enormity of the task; the enormity of the catastrophe; the enormities of the conflict*).

**Enquiry** and **inquiry** are considered interchangeable in the general sense of a question or request for information (*a casual enquiry*). In the specific sense of an official investigation **inquiry** is used, and this spelling is more common for both senses in the US.

Is there a difference between **entitled** and **titled** when referring to the title of a book or work of art? Titled seems to have become more 'correct' in recent years, but there is no basis for this belief. Both have been used in this sense for centuries. The preference for titled may have grown in response to the other meanings of entitled. You can be legally or morally entitled to something — holiday pay, for example, if you've been working for a year. Entitled also refers to those who believe they are deserving of special treatment simply because of who they are (*the entitled son of the president*). In times when people cared more about such things, titled often referred to noble titles (*her titled friends*).

**Entomology** is the study of insects. **Etymology** is the study of word origins or a particular word's origin.

Although envy and jealousy are sometimes used interchangeably to mean a feeling of unhappy longing for the possessions, qualities or success of another, they are not quite the same. **Envy** is directed at a person for what they have and what the person envying desires (*her poise made her the envy of her girlfriends*; *I envy her for the fame she has*). You can also be the object of envy (*his phone made him the envy of his friends*). **Jealousy** can also be envious desires for someone else's things (*they were jealous of his new social group*). But it is also suspicion or fear that one may be replaced as the object of another's affection, something one — theoretically — already possesses (*she couldn't hide her jealousy when he danced with his ex*). So you can jealously guard what you already have.

An **epigram** is a brief, clever and pointed saying ('The only "ism"

Hollywood believes in is plagiarism': Dorothy Parker). An **epigraph** is a quotation or phrase at the beginning of a book, or an inscription on a building. An **epilogue** is the concluding section of a literary work, the match to a prologue at the start. An **epithet** is an adjective or phrase often associated with or presumed to characterise a person or thing (*women who don't give up easily are often given the epithet 'feisty'*). (See **adage**)

**Epistemology** is the philosophical study of the nature and scope of knowledge. **Ontology** is the philosophical study of the nature of existence.

If you are even-tempered, you might be described as **equable**. A climate that doesn't vary much can also be equable. If a deal is fair and just, it is **equitable**.

Often muddled or misused are terms about evasion or delay, possibly because if you avoid acting or answering you are also postponing doing something. **Equivocation** is to use ambiguous language to hide the truth or avoid committing oneself to a position. **Prevarication** is to speak or act in an evasive fashion. **Procrastination** is to delay, defer or postpone. **Vacillation** is frequent alternation between options, wavering or, more generally, hesitation, indecisiveness or uncertainness. The less usual term **prorogation**, from the verb prorogue [proh-rohg], also means to defer or postpone, but usually applies to the discontinuation of a legislative assembly, such as a parliament. (See **ambivalent**, **cunctation**, **waive**)

Something that's **ersatz** is inferior as a substitute (*ersatz butter*) or not real or fake (*ersatz emotion*). **Erstwhile** is literary for former (*erstwhile co-workers*). The near-synonym **sometime** also takes the meaning of 'occasional', particularly in North America, and erstwhile appears to be used in this way infrequently.

**Esoteric** means intended for or likely to be understood by a select group with specialised knowledge, arcane. A less common antonym is **exoteric**, or suitable for public dissemination. **Exotic** means intriguingly out of the ordinary, characteristic of a far-off place, or is a polite term for striptease (*an exotic dancer*). **Existential** means relating to or affirming existence (*an existential threat*) or relating to existentialism.

An **estimable** individual or their behaviour deserves praise or respect (*the estimable proprietor*). Something that's **inestimable** is extremely great or too great to be expressed or appreciated (*inestimable service*) or too great to be calculated (*inestimable storm damage*).

If something happens each day or almost as frequently, or is ordinary or commonplace, it's an **everyday** thing (*an everyday event*; *everyday lives*). Everyday is an adjective that precedes the noun. The adverbial use of daily, **every day**, is two words (*every day he says the same thing*). (See **maybe**)

To be **exact** is to be accurate, thorough, not estimated. An account or person can be exact. As a verb it also means to inflict or obtain. One can exact a confession out of someone or exact revenge upon them. To be **exacting** is to require careful attention (*an exacting approach*), or place great demands on something or someone to get the right result, often in the phrase 'exacting standards'.

To **exalt** is to praise or speak very highly of someone or something (*the website exalted Hitler*) or to raise them to a higher level or rank (*exalt the poor*). To **exult** is to show or feel great joy, often in triumph over another (*exult in the win*).

To **exercise** is to train the body or its muscles, or do something effectively (*exercise judgment*). An exercise is a task, performance or activity. To **exorcise** is to get rid of something bad or oppressive, such as painful memories (*the team exorcised their demons*), from the religious practice — exorcism — of removing an evil spirit believed to be inhabiting an individual. To **exhort** is to urge or encourage someone to do something (*the coach exhorted the players*).

**Exhausting** is extremely tiring (*an exhausting pace of life*). **Exhaustive** is thorough, comprehensive, exhausting all possibilities (*an exhaustive study*).

An **exigency** is a state or situation that requires urgent attention, or that which must be done, often used in plural (*the exigencies of business demand a loosening of working contracts*). **Exigent** means urgent (*exigent needs*) or demanding (*exigent standards*); **exiguous** means scanty, insufficient (*exiguous resources*). An **exegesis** is a critical explanation or interpretation of a literary, academic or religious text (*a full exegesis was expected*).

**Exorbitant** means excessively high, especially in regard to a price or bill. **Exuberant** is full of positive energy and enthusiasm (*an exuberant crowd*), characterised by lavishness and flamboyance (*exuberant style*) or, about plants, growing profusely (*exuberant foliage*).

An **expatriate** [ex-pat-ree-ut] is a citizen who lives abroad. It is frequently shortened to expat, which has no hyphen. It has nothing to do with **patriot**, someone who claims to love their country. To expatriate someone [ex-pat-ree-ate] is to expel or remove them from their native country. To **expatiate** [ex-pay-shee-ate] is to speak or write about something at length or in detail; the original sense of to wander is rare.

A few words are confused by being associated with lack of principle or falseness. **Expedient** refers to something marked by convenience or practicality rather than principle, the noun being expediency (*politically expedient policies*). **Expeditious**, for that matter, means marked by speedy efficiency (*an expeditious solution*). To expedite is to make something happen sooner or faster than it might have. **Specious** means having the appearance of truth but actually being false; or misleading in appearance, especially in attractiveness. **Spurious** is false or not trustworthy, or based on faulty ideas or reasoning. **Fallacious** means based on a fallacy, or deceptive. (See **casuistry**)

**Factitious** means artificial, created by humans rather than by nature (from the Latin for 'made by art'); sham, lacking authenticity. A **factual** account is real, one based on facts. (See **fiction**)

To **faint** is to lose consciousness. A faint hope is weak, not clearly detectable. To **feign** is to pretend or give a false impression of (*she feigned enthusiasm for the movie*). A **feint** is a deceptive move, such as during a fight or to make such a move. It also refers to paper that's printed with faint lines to aid handwriting.

To **falter** is to speak or move uncertainly, with hesitation or coming to a temporary stop (*he didn't falter in his wedding speech*; *she faltered at the graveyard entrance*), to lose strength or purpose (*her will faltered*) or to waver. Occasionally you will see someone described as taking 'haltering steps' or speaking with 'haltering pauses'. A **halter** is a restraining strap that goes around the head of a horse or other animal, so to halter is to restrain. One can halter a development — or **halt** it for that matter — but to use it as a synonym for falter is a mistake. (See **stammer**)

In the 21$^{st}$ century a person can be famous for many things, good and bad, and one man's fame is another woman's infamy. **Famous** means widely known, celebrated, distinguished, being generally used in a positive sense (*famous for its hospitality*) but can be negative (*famous for his parsimony*). Famous occasionally means excellent (*a famous victory*). **Celebrated** is generally used in a positive sense but a newer sense is negative (*celebrated artist*; *celebrated thief*). **Notorious** means well known, generally for a condemnable or scandalous quality (*notorious bank robber*; *notorious publication*). An **infamous** person has a terrible reputation, though the word can also apply to a wicked deed.

**Fanatic** is a judgmental term for a person possessing relentless zeal, especially for an extreme political or religious cause (*religious fanatics*); more casually, it's an extreme enthusiast (*a football fanatic*) or having or showing such enthusiasm (*fanatic audiences*). **Frantic** means affected with fear or anxiety to the point of distraction or hysteria (*frantic with worry*). **Frenetic** means fast and high energy, often in a not-fully-controlled manner (*working at a frenetic pace*).

Something **fantastic** is wonderful or excellent, or is based on fantasy. Something **fantastical** pertains to fantasy, or is bizarre, oddly remarkable, extravagantly fanciful.

A **faun** is a mythological creature, lustful in nature and typically depicted with goat's horns, rear legs and tail. To **fawn** on/upon/over is to court favour with, often with an embarrassing level of attention (*the waiter fawned on her*). Dogs also fawn on their masters, showering them with enthusiastic affection. A young deer is a fawn, and deer fawn when they give birth. Fawn is also a light brown colour.

To **faze** is to unsettle or disconcert (*nothing fazes her*). To **phase** in or out is to introduce or remove in phases — stages of a process or distinguishable periods (*phases of the moon*). Faze and phase are easily and often muddled.

**Febrile** is feverish, either in regards to an illness or an atmosphere (*a febrile state surrounded the palace*). **Feeble** is weak, hopeless. **Futile** means pointless, serving no useful purpose.

**Fecal** relates to faeces (US = feces; faecal is rarely seen). **Feculent** means filthy, foul with sediment, dirt or waste matter. **Fecund** means capable of producing offspring or growth, fertile or intellectually productive. (See **effete, infertile**)

To be **feckless** is to be lacking initiative, purpose or strength of character, or irresponsible. Feck was a regional variant of effect. To be **reckless** is to be rash, not taking due care or consideration. Reck is an obsolete word meaning care or consideration.

A **feud** is a prolonged and bitter dispute, quarrel or state of hostility. Longstanding enemies feud. A **grudge** is a long-lasting case of ill-will or resentment felt towards someone usually due to insult or injury, whether real or imagined. A **vendetta** is a campaign of revenge against someone or a prolonged bitter quarrel with them. It's also a blood feud of a family or tribe seeking vengeance for wrongdoing.

Both **fewer** from **less** mean 'not as many', but fewer applies to things able to be counted individually — and always of people. Less applies to things that can't be counted individually, as well as time, money, distance and weight. *In less than 100 days* rather than *fewer than 100 days*. If a sentence takes a singular verb — four minutes is . . ., 5 kilometres is . . ., $1 million is . . ., 40 kilograms is . . ., 30 percent is . . . — then you can use less; countable things usually take a plural verb and so use fewer. If it's a target or if numbers provide the size of a quantity — 50 runs, 20 points, 100 pages, 1200 words, 20 calories — you can use less. It is always one less bicycle or apple or elephant than previously, not fewer.

**Fiction** is literature, usually in prose form, written for love and sometimes money (*historical fiction*). A fiction is also something that is invented or untrue, often because it serves a purpose (*their happy home life is a fiction*). Something **fictitious** is not real, is invented, created in the imagination, but the word can mean not genuine or feigned (*a fictitious backstory; his affection was fictitious*). Something that's **fictional** has been created for the purpose of fiction (*a fictional character*). Both it and **fictive** generally have more neutral connotations (*a fictive view of his family*). (See **factitious**)

Two expressions from the Old Testament. As a metaphor, a **fig leaf** is something, often makeshift and obvious, that attempts to camouflage another thing that's embarrassing or morally dubious (*the policy was merely a fig leaf for the government's guilt over tax cuts*). It is what covers the genitals in traditional paintings or sculpture and arrived via the Bible's 'Genesis' chapter courtesy of Adam and Eve, who hid theirs with leaves from a fig tree after eating the forbidden fruit. An **olive branch**, by comparison, is an offer or gesture that indicates a desire for peace or conciliation (*the government extended an olive branch to the strikers*). It again stems from 'Genesis', this time the dove bringing back a branch after the great flood, seen as a symbol of peace after God's watery punishment of the world.

**Filial** means of a son, though sometimes of a daughter (*filial loyalty*). **Philately** is stamp collecting.

If you are listing a series of points in sentences, use '**first**', 'second' and so on (*First, we must get buy-in from staff. Second, we must carry out the plan*). Writing '**firstly**', 'secondly' etc. is regarded as unnecessary by modern style guides, if not completely inelegant once you get to 'eighthly'.

Commonly mistaken are flaunt and flout. **Flaunt** — rhymes with taunt — means to show off oneself or one's possessions arrogantly (*flaunted his wealth*; *flaunting themselves*). To **flout** — rhymes with shout — is to openly ignore (*they flouted the rules*). The word may come from the Dutch for 'to play the flute at' in derision.

To **flesh** out is to give greater substance or detail to something or expand (*he fleshed out his plan*). To **flush** out is to make public or force out into the open, as of game birds or those who want to remain hidden (*the move was intended to flush out the rebels*).

A **flier** or **flyer** is a person who flies on board an aircraft (*a frequent flier*) or upfront as pilot (*an experienced flier*). It's also something or someone that's travelling quickly (*a flier on the left wing*); a misdirected hit of a ball, as in golf; a flying start (*she's off to a flier*). A high-flier or high-flyer is a person with excellent chances for promotion within a company or industry. Flier is probably more commonly used than flyer in the US (where it also means a speculative venture, as in 'she took a flier in a tech company'), and vice versa in the Commonwealth countries. However, flyer is more commonly used to mean a promotional leaflet, usually a single sheet, in most countries.

A **floe** is a flat segment of floating ice. Everything else to do with liquid or other things moving smoothly and freely is **flow**.

**Flotsam** is the floating wreckage of a ship or its cargo. Broadly speaking, it is also used about things and people, such as asylum seekers, that have been discarded or disregarded (*the flotsam of conflict*). **Jetsam** is the floating parts of a ship or its cargo that have been thrown overboard to reduce its weight, or jettisoned. To **jettison** now also means to cast off something regarded as unwanted or burdensome. The less common term **lagan** is jetsam distinguished by having a buoy attached so it can be relocated, or that placed or found on the ocean floor. The phrase flotsam and jetsam means miscellaneous material. (See **debris**)

It's not surprising many confuse flounder and founder, as they sound so similar and both carry the sense of failure. To **flounder** means to struggle helplessly or flop about to regain one's balance, especially in water or mud. It is commonly used to mean to struggle (*she floundered for the right words*; *he was floundering in the course*) or about business (*a floundering economy*). To **founder** — the sense of sinking to the bottom is central — means to fail or collapse (*talks foundered*). A foundering ship is one that is taking on water and about to sink. Founder can also mean, of a horse, to stumble or become lame.

To **forbear** is to resist, refrain from or be tolerant or patient in the face of provocation. A **forebear** is an ancestor. (See **descendant**)

Some traditionalists insist that **forensic** relates only to that which is appropriate for courts of law (it comes from the Latin for 'of the forum', 'public'), but it also now has the sense of scientific methods applied to the investigation of crime, and is gaining a wider sense of such detailed analysis, whether legally intentioned or not (*forensic accounting*).

The **foreword** of a book is a short introduction, often by someone other than the author. **Forward(s)** means towards the front, in the front, in the future, or progressing (*forward thinking*), bold (*such forward behaviour*). A forward is a player in sports teams whose job is to attack. To forward is to send on. (See **backward**)

To **forgo** is to do without, abstain from, particularly something pleasant, its past being forwent and past participle being forgone. The misspelling of forego is becoming common, though this would lead us to foregone, which means preceded, the verb forego having gone the way of the pterodactyl, so is best avoided. (See **bygone**)

**Formally** means in a formal manner, or officially (*formally welcomed*). **Formerly** is previously or having been at one time (*formerly a police officer*). (See **former**)

If something is the **former**, it is the first of two things mentioned (*given a choice of fighting or being court-martialled, he opted for the former*). If there are more than two, avoid the temptation to use former and latter, and opt for the first, the second, third, last and so on, or repeat the thing itself. Former also relates to something earlier in time or in the past (*a shadow of his former glory*) or having been something previously (*a former diplomat*). (See **better, formally, latter**)

A **fount** of wisdom is a figurative source, usually a person, whose knowledge of useful things is impressive. The phrase is often used in a literary or humorous context. Fount is a back-formation of fountain, as mount from mountain. It is exceedingly common to hear 'a font of knowledge'. A **font** is a receptacle, most commonly containing baptismal water or that which has been blessed, or a reservoir for other liquids, so unless you want the sticklers on your back stick with fount.

A **fracas** [fra-kah] is a noisy, disorderly fight or quarrel, or a brawl. A **furore** [fyoo-ror-ee or fyoo-ror] is an outbreak of public indignation or excitement in reaction to something (*a furore over the new immigration laws*; *the play caused a furore*). Furor is the common spelling in the US.

**Frangible** means capable of being broken into pieces (*frangible bullets*) or fragile. **Fungible** is easy to trade, exchange or replace, particularly in regard to financial assets or commodities (*money is fungible*). **Tangible** things are real (*a tangible threat*), concrete, capable of being touched (*his fear was almost tangible*).

Something that's **fraught** causes or is filled with anxiety or tension (*the shopping trip was fraught*; *a fraught relationship*). Fraught with means full of or burdened with (*fraught with peril*). **Wrought** is an archaic past participle of work meaning, of metal, created or shaped (*wrought iron fence*). It is applied to other things made or fashioned (*the project wrought change*; *a well-wrought script*). It's also commonly used, particularly in the US, in an apparent extension of 'wrought havoc' from wreak, to mean bring about or inflict (*suffering wrought on that nation*) or fraught's sense of burdened with (*wrought with trouble*). **Overwrought** means too elaborate or complicated (*an overwrought finale*); in a state of being highly upset, anxious or nervously excited (*overwrought at the prospect of the visit*). Wrought-up is also used in the US for an excited state. (See **wreak**)

To **freeze** is to turn into ice or cool to a low temperature; to become motionless; or to cease functioning, often temporarily, as of a computer. It is also the act of holding in a fixed state, or a period of very cold weather. A **frieze** is a term in art meaning an ornamented or sculpted band on a wall, or one of wallpaper, especially near the ceiling. It's also the upper part of a classical building supported by columns between the architrave and cornice.

Some useful words about composure or reserve can be jumbled, all of which come to us from French. **Froideur** is coolness, aloofness, reserve between people, often sudden in appearance. **Hauteur** is arrogance or proud haughtiness of manner. **Sangfroid**, however, is more positive. Literally meaning 'cold blood', it is coolness, composure or level-headedness, especially when under extreme pressure. (See **amour propre, insouciance**)

Is there a difference between **frowzy/frowsy** and **frowsty**? These redolent words can both mean smelling musty, fusty, stale, like something has hasn't been washed or aired in a while. Frowsty suggests a warm, stuffy atmosphere. But frowzy is also used to mean a dirty, unkempt appearance, such as in one's clothes, hair or complexion.

The adjective **fulsome** is the site of many a minor word-related skirmish. Some fervently believe that its general modern meaning, of being flattering to an excessive degree, so unpleasantly ingratiating, should be the only one used. It's a useful distinction: too much rather than a lot. But the word originally meant plentiful, abundant — full + some — and many have come again to use it that way. To avoid confusion, as with **moot**, **nonplussed** and **disinterested** (words that might be similarly regarded as 'skunked'), it may be preferable to use another term, such as generous or overdone or smarmy. (See **egregious**)

For writers outside the US, the distinction between **further** and **furthest** for metaphorical distances and **farther** and **farthest** for literal distance is disappearing. Further and furthest now provide everything you need. In the US, however, the distinction appears to be becoming stronger. While the two have previously been interchangeable when discussing distance, increasingly farther is being preferred for distance (*farther east*) and further when the ideas are about addition (*further questions*).

# G

A **gaffe** is a mistake or blunder (*gaffe-prone speech*). It is frequently mistakenly written, even in headlines, as gaff. A **gaff** is a fishing hook, a nautical spar, or UK slang for home (*this is my gaff*). A **gaffer** is the chief electrician on a film set, or UK slang for an old man or a boss.

**Gainsay**, which is generally used in a formal or literary context, means to deny, contradict, dispute or oppose. It has nothing to do with gaining anything and is instead related to speaking *against* something. Think against-say and you'll be fine.

A **gambit** is the opening move in a game or manoeuvre, particularly one that attempts to gain an advantage. It comes from the Italian for 'tripping up the heels' from *gamba*, leg. Originally it was a bold move in chess before being deployed more widely. The **gamut** is the range or full extent of something (*the character runs the gamut of emotions from party to pity*), and also applies to a full set of musical notes or the range of an instrument, coming from Latin *gamma-ut*, representing a historical scale. (See **ambit**)

To **garner** is to gather or collect (*to garner their approval*). To **garnish** means two almost opposite things, to add to or take away. It is to decorate or embellish, usually in regard to food (*an edible garnish*). And it means to seize money from someone to pay a debt, usually through a deduction on wages or to serve notice that you intend to seize money on behalf of a debtor (*his wages were garnished*).

There is considerable crossover between geek and nerd. A **geek** is an intelligent but often socially inept or unfashionable person, or someone of considerable and obsessive but narrow knowledge (*a computer geek*). The term has been reclaimed as positive to some degree in recent decades, particularly in the Silicon Valley era. Non-geeks can geek out — get detail-obsessive — over a new superhero movie, for example. In the US, a geek is also a certain type of circus or carnival performer with an act. A **nerd** often shares the unfashionable, introverted and obsessive qualities of the geek but also has the reputation of being exceptionally studious (*I was a nerd at school*). A **wonk** is a person who has valuable but arcane knowledge in one area, particularly politics (*a policy wonk*).

**Gender** and **sex** are often used interchangeably in the 21$^{st}$ century, though traditionally gender refers to the state of being male or female based on social, psychological and cultural differences rather than biological ones, one's sex, and the words still maintain those meanings. But it is now commonly used to mean sexual identity, including those that fall outside the binary of male and female. Gender in grammar refers to a class of nouns and related words often distinguished by word inflections or articles, such as German *die*, *das* and *der*. Sex also refers commonly to sexual activity, or it is a verb meaning to determine the sex of something or someone (*to sex a chick*, for instance). (See **cis**, **LGBT**)

**Genteel** means refined or polite, often in an affected way. **Gentile** is not Jewish, or not Mormon. **Gentle** is considerate and tender or mild of disposition. Said of something physical, it means not severe or steep or sudden (*a gentle hill*; *a gentle ride*).

**Gravitas**, generally applied to a person, means exuding dignity and seriousness and so creating feelings of trust and respect (*he has both the insight and gravitas needed to be head of the country*). **Gravity**, beyond the fundamental physical force, means significance or seriousness (*I understand the gravity of what I am taking on*), or dignity or solemnity of manner (*the passage was read with suitable gravity*).

**Grisly** [griz-lee] means inspiring horror, fear or disgust (*a grisly sight*). **Gristly** [griss-lee] means composed of or containing a large amount of gristle, as of meat. **Grizzly** [griz-lee] is grizzled, streaked with grey, as of hair; a type of North American brown bear; or complaining and crying, as of a young child (*grizzly with colic*).

The hairs on the back and neck, particularly of a dog, are its **hackles**. Metaphorically, to make someone's hackles rise is to anger them. To **heckle** is to harass, usually a stage performer, with comments and interjections.

To **hanker** for something is to have a strong desire to do it or have it, especially in the phrase 'to hanker after/for/to do something'. It's used in the phrase 'to have a hankering for'. To **hunker** is to crouch, squat, hunch over. To hunker down is to apply oneself dedicatedly to one task or location, or hold stubbornly to an attitude or decision (*the White House hunkered down on the deal*).

**Haptic** relates to the sense of touch, especially in regards to technology interfaces or virtual reality (*haptic feedback*), or means tactile. **Phatic** relates to speech that has a social or emotion-related function rather than informational (*How are you going?*).

A **harbinger** [HAR-bin-jə] is someone or something that heralds or foreshadows the arrival of something else (*the cold rains were harbingers of autumn*) or the forerunner of something (*the peaceful protests were harbingers of more violent demonstrations*). It is also a verb (*the fireworks harbingered the start of celebrations*). From twelfth-century French meaning a host, it came to stand for someone who went ahead to find lodging, and so a herald.

Many people casually say that someone who died had had a heart attack, but strictly speaking this is not correct. A **heart attack**, also known as a **myocardial infarction**, happens when blood flow decreases or stops to a part of the heart. It's often due to one of the major coronary arteries becoming blocked, usually as a result of coronary artery disease. The heart muscle might start to die because of a lack of oxygen arriving through the blood. Symptoms can be immediate and intense, or gradual: chest pain is the most common. A **cardiac arrest** is when the heart stops pumping blood around the body and the person stops breathing normally. Many cardiac arrests happen as a result of a heart attack, because the person having one can develop a dangerous, irregular heart rhythm — **arrhythmia** — that leads to arrest. The American Heart Association says a heart attack is a 'circulation' problem and cardiac arrest is an 'electrical' problem. Regardless of whichever someone is suffering, call your emergency number.

A **hermetic** seal on a bottle is airtight, and so a hermetic life or society is one insulated from external influences. Hermetic also means difficult to understand because it's abstruse or esoteric (*hermetic writings*). **Heuristic** methods of teaching and learning are based on discovery, trial and error, and problem-solving strategies based on past experience. A heuristic computer program is one that can learn and solve problems; in teaching, heuristic learning comes by way of students discovering for themselves. A heuristic can be a method or argument, or rule of thumb. Heuristics is the study of such techniques.

**Hermeneutics** is the theory and study of interpreting texts; **hermeneutic** means explanatory. (See **esoteric**)

To **hew** is to carve a shape out of wood or other materials, or shape metaphorically (*hew out a life*). In the US it also means to conform or adhere (*he hewed to a certain way of thinking*), apparently from following a cutting line. A **hue** is a shade of colour. It can also mean character or appearance (*wannabes of all political hues*).

The distinction between historic and historical may be a lost cause, given how often online it is used incorrectly. **Historic** means having great or lasting importance, usually due to association with significant events in history, so having a value for commemoration (*politicians too timid to drive for historic change*), whereas **historical** is that which happened in the past, regardless of its importance (*the historical society meets next week*). (See **classic**, **economic**)

A **hoard** is a store of something; to hoard is to amass such a store. A **horde** is a loose gathering of people (*a horde of followers*) or ancient warriors (*Mongol hordes*).

The **hoi polloi** is a mildly derogatory term for ordinary people. Even though it's Ancient Greek for 'the many', the hoi polloi is common English usage. The term is sometimes confused with **hoity-toity**, which has almost the opposite meaning of snobbish or superior in attitude (*hoity-toity neighbours*).

To **home** in is to move closer towards a target (*missiles homed in on the bunker*) or to focus or move towards an objective (*home in on the details*). It's not hone in on, a very common error. There are no honing pigeons. To **hone** is to make sharper (*hone the knife blade*) or refine (*hone your manuscript*).

A **homonym** (Latin: same name) has the same pronunciation and perhaps spelling as another word but a different meaning and origin, such as row (of seats) and row (a boat). Broadly speaking, a homonymic word could be a homophone or a homograph. A **homophone** (Latin: same sound) sounds the same as another word but has a different meaning, origin and spelling, such as peace and piece. A **homograph** (Latin: written same) has the same spelling but different meaning, origin and perhaps pronunciation, such as bow (of an archer) and bow (as to applause).

The adverb **hopefully** traditionally means 'in a hopeful manner' (*the priest looked hopefully on his congregation*). But far more often it is used to mean 'it is to be hoped', i.e. to convey the hope of the speaker. Adverbs modify verbs, adjectives and other adverbs. They are also widely used, in what is called a sentence adverb or disjunct, to comment on an entire sentence — 'Hopefully, the rain will stop soon.' The speaker is hoping the rain will stop. Many decry such usage and some even look askance at any sentence adverbs. Others say some are fine; fortunately, sadly, clearly, regrettably can be paraphrased as 'it is fortunate/sad/clear/regrettable'. Hopefully is regarded as odd by the some-are-okay crowd in that this is not possible, or that it's not clear who or what expressed the hope. Some will even change it to 'it is hoped that'. It seems unnecessary to do this — the meaning that's intended is perfectly clear and widely accepted. The same goes for **thankfully, mercifully, admittedly**. It is, however, still useful to prefer **regrettably** rather than **regretfully** as a sentence adverb when suggesting something that gives rise to regret (*regrettably, the show was cancelled*). The latter suggests feeling or showing regret and belongs in formal letters declining, for example, an invitation to your ex-wife's wedding. As with all sentence adverbs, if there is the possibility of ambiguity or if its arguable use is likely to distract the reader, consider recasting the sentence.

The prefix **hyper** indicates a level over, beyond, above normal, as in hyperactive and hyper-articulate. In casual use, hyper, when applied to a person as a character trait, is highly strung; in a temporary state, a hyper person, particularly a child, is overstimulated, easily excited, unable to concentrate. **Hypo**, which appears less often outside technical use, indicates under, beneath, down, below normal, as in hypoallergenic (of a substance, less likely to cause an allergic reaction), hypoxia (low levels of oxygen in the body or an environment) or hypodermic (beneath the skin). **Hypochondria** is an abnormal concern with one's health to the point of anxiety or depression, especially thinking one is suffering all manner of serious illnesses. The word comes from Greek via Latin for the region below the breastbone, where such anxiety was believed to originate. Hypo is a frequently used abbreviation for a hypodermic needle, or hypoglycaemic, i.e. having low levels of glucose in the bloodstream.

# I

In medicine, **iatrogenic** relates to illness caused by a doctor or medical treatment (*iatrogenic complications*). If it's **idiopathic** it relates to illness or a condition of unknown cause (*idiopathic arthritis*).

An **icon** is a person or thing that attracts widespread admiration (*the late music icon David Bowie*) or is a symbol of an ideal (*the open road is an icon of freedom*). Outside of its meanings in art (religious image) and computing (screen image or symbol), the word is exhausted through overuse. Similarly, **iconic**, which, rather than referring to something that strongly represents a particular time or set of attitudes, has come to be applied to every person or brand that is reasonably known, has some track record or is slightly distinctive. Use with restraint. An **iconoclast** is someone who challenges established ideas or institutions, originally being someone who opposed the use of religious images in worship and destroyed them. **Iconography** is the use or study of form and symbol in the visual arts, or the visual images associated with a person, group, movement etc.

**Idle** [eye-dil] is lazy or without work. An **idol** [eye-dil] is the image of a god, a false god or someone who is adored by fans (*movie idol*). An **idyll** [id-il] is an extremely happy, carefree or picturesque time, place or experience. Or it's a short poem or prose piece describing an idealised rural or romantic theme.

Poor old **impact**: it never gets taken seriously. Its use as a verb outside of meteors and shells landing to much devastation is widely frowned upon by traditionalists, far more than the thousands of other back-formations from nouns. Even though impact has been used as a verb for centuries — before it was first noted as a noun — and in the sense of 'impact on' for at least half a century. The earliest uses of the word related to the body (*impacted bowels* and the like). The distaste towards impact seems to have become stronger when the meaning of 'to have an impact on' changed from actual collision to figurative effect. Its use increased in the last decades of the twentieth century, particularly in commercial writing (*impacted the bottom line*) and it gained the status of jargon. Similarly disliked by many are the use as verbs of **leverage**, **action**, **task**, **grow** (a business), and even **enthuse** and **enhance**. If you happen to feel no strong dislike for 'impacted upon', it might pay to avoid the term 'impactful'.

Frequently confused, even by careful users, are **imply** and **infer**. To imply is to suggest: I imply something in what I say. To infer is to deduce: you infer something from what I said. An implication is made by one person, speaking, for example, and an inference by another person, listening. It's tempting to believe that the confusion is sometimes deliberate. To reject an inference is not to accept an interpretation; to apologise for an inference, even if it is the only one possible, is to be perhaps sorry for what was taken from a statement or news story rather than what it might have implied — and can be denied. If the logic of the sentence is clear, the reader should be able to add 'to be drawn' after inference. (See **adduce**)

Something that's **imprudent** is unwise or indiscreet, the opposite of prudent (*an imprudent email*). If it's **impudent** it's rude, cheeky, not showing due respect (*an impudent smile*).

Commonly misused is **inchoate**, which means imperfectly formed, in an early stage of development, partial, incipient (*inchoate fears*). It does not mean **incoherent**, which is lacking in cohesion, order or clarity, or just hard to understand (*incoherent ramblings*).

An **incredible** story is one that's so extraordinary it's hard to believe, or is just marvellous or amazing. An **incredulous** person is unwilling or unable to believe something is true, or is sceptical. An incredulous look or stare is expressive of disbelief. (See **credible**)

If something — an argument, or a castle — can't be defended from clever or sustained attack, it is regarded as **indefensible**. But indefensible also carries the sense of inexcusable or unforgivable, such as an action or a point of view that can never be justified, at least in the mind of the accuser. Be clear if you think an idea is weak or misleading, unacceptable or just plain wrong. The word **undefendable** also exists, and can be applied to debate and war (*undefendable actions, undefendable borders*), but it's less common.

**Indigent** means poor or needy (*indigent artists*), or is a needy or destitute person or people (*homeless indigents*). Don't confuse this with **diligent**, which means hardworking, or **indolent**, which is lazy; in medicine, indolent means slow to progress and usually painless (*an indolent ulcer*). If you are **indignant** you are annoyed or resentful about wrong or unjust treatment. **Redolent** means fragrant, or suggestive or bringing to mind, such as a memory (*redolent of past glories*).

**Infertile** means not able to reproduce (*the couple had infertility issues*) or unproductive, such as land (*infertile soil*). **Impotent** means lacking in strength or vigour or unable to act (*an impotent government*) or, of a male, unable to engage in sexual intercourse because of an inability to achieve and sustain an erection. **Sterile** means unable to produce offspring (*sterile mosquito larvae*), free from germs (*a sterile laboratory*) or lacking in creative or intellectual stimulation or producing no results (*a sterile working environment*).

Perhaps you're looking for a word meaning coolly indifferent or perfectly chilled behaviour. Two of these come from French originally and one from Italian, if that's any surprise. **Insouciance** is blithe or lighthearted lack of concern, or indifference. **Nonchalance** is casual calmness, lack of concern or apparent indifference. **Sprezzatura**, a less commonly used term in English, is the art of making perfect conduct or artistic endeavour appear to be without effort or much thought. (See **froideur**)

Into or in to? On to or onto? **Into**, a preposition expressing movement, change of state etc., is widely accepted as standard English. In theory there is a difference between a phrasal verb such as hand in + to (*she handed the essay in to her teacher*) and into as a standalone preposition (*the argument turned into a full-on brawl*). In everyday use the distinction is blurred, and mostly passes unnoticed. **Onto**, however, while common in the US, is not regarded as standard British English (onto also has a specialist mathematical meaning we don't need to worry about) and should always be written as two words. Even if the trend to onto is irresistible, the phrasal-verb distinction is worth preserving (*she climbed onto the roof of the car; the discussion moved on to a new topic*).

Be careful in your use of the words **ironic** or **ironically**. Irony is not having too many spoons when all you need is a knife, as the song goes. It is, as the comedian noted, when it turns out a spoon would have done fine. Situational irony is when there is a sharp or poignant contrast or discrepancy, often humorous, between what is expected to happen and what happens. Verbal irony is when someone says something but means something else, usually the opposite, often in a sarcastic or mocking way. In dramatic irony, the audience or the other characters know something that a character does not. To be precise, and to avoid an argument with traditionalists, check you don't mean: in an unexpected juxtaposition, amusingly, interestingly, inadvertently, coincidentally, timely, untimely, conveniently, conversely, fortunately, unfortunately, serendipitously, tenuously, thankfully, unexpectedly, poignantly, oddly, weirdly, strangely, funnily, paradoxically, perversely, spookily. (See **sarcastic**)

**Its** means that which belongs to it. **It's** is a contraction for it is or it has. If it is short for it is or it has, write it's. If it isn't, write its. This is a surprisingly common error.

# J

Just as we previously believed human personalities were strongly indicated by the four humours, it came to be thought that the planets — that is, the classical planets the ancients could see without modern astronomical equipment — could influence us also. Three were most commonly roped in to help. Those who were **jovial**, i.e. from Jove so born under Jupiter, were cheerful and good-humoured. Those born under Mercury were **mercurial** — clever, lively and quick-witted but often volatile and changeable in temperament. **Saturnine** folks, influenced by Saturn, were morose, sluggish and taciturn, and tended to be sardonic. (See **choleric, sarcastic**)

A **junction** is a joining point, or the act or process or boundary of that which is being joined. A **juncture** is a point in time, or the act or state of being joined (*at this juncture, the report will not be released*).

# L

Traditionally, to **labour** a point was to spend too much time explaining or arguing it, and to **belabour** someone was to attack them physically or verbally (*don't belabour your elders*), but it is now common to hear of people belabouring a point or two.

To **lacerate** is to tear or make deep cuts in, especially skin or flesh, or to distress greatly, as through criticism. To **macerate** is to soften or break up by placing in liquid, especially food, or to cause to grow thin or weak. **Masticate** is a fancy word meaning to chew.

**Lachrymal** relates to tears, weeping or the tear glands. **Lachrymose** means tearful or tending to produce tears. **Lapidary** has nothing to do with crying but means sharply defined (*as in facial features*); marked by concision, precision or refinement; related to precious stones or the working of them; or engraved in stone. A lapidary is also someone who works with precious stones.

**Lackadaisical** means lacking interest, enthusiasm or determination, or simply lazy. **Lacklustre** means lacking in vitality or excitement, or unimpressive. If you're talking about hair it means not shiny. **Lassitude** is a state or feeling of weariness or listlessness. **Lax** is not adequately disciplined or careful. Of limbs, bowels or speech sounds, it means loose or relaxed. (See **laxative**)

**Largesse** — in the US the spelling largess is also used — is generosity in giving, particularly money or gifts, liberal giving, or that which is given. The word is often used with at least a hint of judgment, or with the sense that the benevolence is ostentatious.

**Latter** is often used when **last** would be more appropriate. When you are highlighting the second of two things mentioned, use latter. (*He's a liar and a hypocrite, but it's the latter I really object to.*) If you're highlighting the first of two things, use former. Latter is also used to refer to something closer to the end than the beginning (*the latter half of 2016*) and more recent times (*the car's run well in latter years*). Use last when you're referring to the final of three or more things mentioned. (*I can't swim, dance or play piano, though it's the last that disappoints me the most.*) If referring to any other, use first or second etc. Last is also used for the most immediate occurrence (*last Wednesday*). **Latest** can be used for the most recent in a series (*her latest hobby*). (See **better**, **former**)

To **lead** [leed] is to guide from the front. The most important husky, for example, is the lead. It's also another word for an animal leash. **Lead** [led] is a metallic element, and figuratively something heavy (*my feet felt like lead*). To be **led** [led] is to be guided from the front. In the US, the **lede** [leed], an alteration of the frontal sense of lead, is the introductory sentence(s) of a news story. To bury the lede is to fail to use the most interesting or important element in the introduction.

**Leeway** is a margin of freedom or ability to move, latitude, or safety.

It was originally the downwind drift of a ship. **Leverage** is power to influence to gain an advantage, originally being the advantage or force gained by use of a lever. In finance terms it's the ratio of debt to equity. (See **impact**)

**LGBT** is an initialism (see **acronym**) for the communities of lesbian, gay, bisexual and transgender people, though some object to trans inclusion for combining gender identity with sexual orientation. Others prefer to include queer, intersex (and asexual) people with the initialisms LGBTQI or LGBTIQ or LGBTIQA, or LGBT+ to include the spectrum. It pays to ask how someone identifies rather than assuming. (See **cis**, **gender**)

Historically, **libel** was defamation — statements that damage someone's reputation — published in print or online form, i.e. had some permanence. **Slander** was spoken and so more transient. Many countries no longer have a distinction between the two forms.

If an activity is **licit**, it is lawful, permissible. Its opposite is the more common **illicit**. Something that is illicit is not always against the law, however, and may simply be something that society frowns upon, most commonly an illicit extramarital affair. If it's against the law, it's **illegal**. Something that's **unlawful**, meanwhile, might simply contravene the laws of a country or the rules in a specific context, as under a sporting code.

**Lie** and **lay** are much confused, and we can't just blame Bob Dylan. Writers have been double-checking themselves for centuries. The present and past of to **lie** — to tell an untruth — is simple enough: she lies; she lied; she has lied; she was lying. To **lie** — to be horizontal — is trickier: he lies down on the bed; he lay down on the bed; he has lain down on the bed; he was lying on the bed. An object or dead person is the same — a body lies in a coffin; a body lay in the coffin; a body has lain in the coffin; a body is lying in the coffin. As does something that exists or is situated — the house lies empty; it lay empty; it has lain empty for years; it has been lying empty for years. To **lay** — to place something or someone down — is written like this: he lay the gun down; he laid the gun down; he has laid the gun down; he was laying the gun down. She lay a hand on his arm; she laid a hand on his arm; she had laid a hand on his arm; her hand was laying on his arm.

Frequently misused are words related to light and making lighter in terms of weight. **Lighting** is luminous objects and their effect. **Lightening** is reducing the weight of something. **Lightning** is the electricity bolt from clouds. Don't insert an 'e' if it has anything to do with lifting or effort.

If you are tempted to use the word **limerence**, it's a term coined in the 1970s by a psychologist that means a feeling of romantic infatuation for someone with the strong desire to have it reciprocated. Such a desire is limerent. Limerence is deemed the first state of romantic love, and its departure suggests a transition to another state (*the state of limerence lasts until reality breaks in*). **Liminal**, on that subject, relates to a transitional state or on the threshold of something (*in this worrying liminal phase of politics*). The noun is liminality.

If a handshake is **limp** it lacks stiffness, firmness or energy. If a body is limp it is without strength or movement. To limp is to walk with a slow and uneven step, a limp, due to injury or ailment. To limp is also to progress in a faltering fashion, such as a damaged boat (*to limp into port*) or an economy (*limping along*). **Limpid** means transparent, unclouded of liquid (*limpid pools*) and eyes (*a limpid gaze*); easily understood, simple in style (*limpid prose*); another meaning is calm, peaceful (*a limpid sunset*). A **limpet** is a marine mollusc with a conical shell that clings tightly to rocks, or type of explosive device fixed to its target, especially limpet mines. Used in comparisons, it's a person or thing that clings tightly to another (*that child is a limpet*).

**Lissome** means nimble, lithe, gracefully slender. **Winsome** means pleasant, agreeable, charming in an open and innocent manner. **Whimsical** means playful or fanciful, especially in a lightly humorous way, or capricious.

To take something **literally** is to accept its literal sense — i.e. based on fact or without exaggeration, the strict meaning of words, or word for word — rather than its metaphorical sense. It's used to emphasise the truth or accuracy of statement or description (*there were literally thousands of people waiting*). Or you could translate something literally: flea market is directly from French — *marché aux puces*, apparently from the fleas attracted by old goods. The definition that people most object to, even more so its inclusion in dictionaries, is to use literally to mean figuratively. Or for emphasis or exaggeration when something that can't be actually true. 'I literally died', when you didn't; 'The holiday specials literally walked out of the door'. One meaning contradicts the other, the argument goes. But why, goes another, focus on literally when we usually aren't so hard on intensifiers such as really, truly, in fact (*in fact the place was a bomb site*), totally (*totally bored to death*) or honestly (*honestly blew our minds*)? It has been used this way for literally centuries, and it's doubtful that it's confused one person. Still, it's probably best to steer clear unless your apparently figurative use is actually true and she literally did fall on the floor in laughter.

**Littoral** has nothing to do with literal. It means of or relating to the shore of a body of water (*the littoral zone is close to the shore*) or the area between high and low tides. **Riparian** means relating to or located on the bank of a natural watercourse, such as a river, or sometimes a lake.

A **load** is the weight or burden that a human or an animal bears, or a structure such as an arch, or a vehicle. It's also casual language for 'a lot'. A **lode** is a deposit of metal ore in the earth, or a rich source of something. It's surprisingly common to see 'mother load' written in newspapers, though to be generous some of these might be attempted parenting puns.

Words to watch are **loath**, meaning unwilling or reluctant (*I am loath to reveal the truth about their relationship*), and **loathe**, to strongly dislike or feel disgust for (*she loathes me, but I'm not sure why*). (See **callous, mucous**)

**Loose** and **lose** are confused surprisingly often, usually the writing of loose where lose should be. **Lose** [looz] mainly means to not win, the noun being loss and the past tense lost (*they went on to lose the game, the loss being the fourth of the season*). It also means to be deprived of something, misplace it, to fail to keep or hold. You can also lose faith, face or your appetite, lose a child, weight or your temper, lose your place, your mind, a stalker or an argument, lose a baby before birth, an opportunity or money. **Loose** [loos] means untethered or not tight in place (*the boat came loose*), free from confinement (*a bull on the loose*) or restraint (*loose morals*), imprecise (*loose legislation*) and not completely solid (*loose ground*), among other uses. It can be used as a verb, in the sense of setting free (*to loose the hounds*) or let fly (*loose an arrow*).

**Lubricious** behaviour is that showing or displaying sexual desire, especially in an unpleasant way, lecherous. It also means smooth, slippery as with an oily film. **Oleaginous** is oily, but also ingratiating in manner, obsequious. **Unctuous** behaviour is excessively flattering or over-friendly in an unappealing manner; unctuous also means greasy, soapy or oily in texture. (See **lugubrious, meretricious**)

**Lucrative** means profitable. **Ludicrous** means absurd.

**Lugubrious** means appearing or sounding sad, serious or gloomy (*his lugubrious expression*; *such lugubrious music*). A lugubrious man — it's usually applied to males — might also be one of few words, but in that case he is also **laconic**. **Salubrious** means healthy, wholesome (*salubrious mountain air*); or respectable, pleasant (*a salubrious suburb*). Its antonym is insalubrious. **Salacious** gossip appeals to interest in sexual matters. (See **lubricious**)

**Luxuriant** means marked by thick and heavy growth (*a luxuriant head of hair*), plentiful and lush (*luxuriant greenery*), or elaborate and flowery (*luxuriant prose*). **Luxurious** is expensive, opulent, characterised by luxury, self-indulgent (*luxurious day spa*).

**A magnate** is a wealthy, powerful and probably influential business person. A **magnet** is an object producing a magnetic field and capable of attracting other objects of certain metals, or something that attracts people or things (*a publicity-magnet*).

**Malicious** means full of malice or spite, intending harm (*a malicious attack*; *a malicious email*). **Pernicious** means tending to cause great harm, especially in a gradual way or one not readily noticed. (See **benign**)

To **malinger** is to feign illness to avoid work or a task (*they were suspected of malingering*). To **philander**, usually said of a man, is to have casual sex with women, especially those who are not his committed partner. It appears most commonly as a noun: philandering, philanderer (*her father was a philanderer*).

A **mantel** is a mantelpiece, that is, a shelf or structure above or around a fireplace. A **mantle** is a type of cloak or shawl, a covering or layer (*mantle of snow*) and a responsibility that passes from one to another (*taking up the mantle of leadership*). It's also the layer of a planet between the crust and core.

**Marital** means related to marriage. While sometimes it might seem warlike, that's **martial**, which relates to things of war, the military and fighting (*martial society*; *martial arts*). A **marshal** is a military officer or high public official; as a verb, it means to gather or arrange in order.

Some traditionalists claim a distinction between masterful and masterly. **Masterful**, it is said, means powerful, dominating (*a masterful bearing*); **masterly** means showing great skill, very accomplished (*masterly technique*). In practice, both are used to refer to skill, and the rationale behind the claim is regarded by authorities as thin. There are many other words to use.

**Material** [ma-TEER-ee-əl] is substance out of which something is made, or cloth or fabric. It relates to the physical realm (*the material world*) or is significant or important (*material facts*). It's information for a project such as a book (*research material*) or the substance of a performer's act, particularly a comedian. **Materiel** [ma-teer-ee-EL], sometimes written matériel, is the equipment and supplies of a military organisation.

There is no difference between using **maximum** or **maximal** as an adjective for the greatest, highest, largest number or amount permitted or possible; the former has been used in this way since the eighteenth century. The noun is maximum only. It can also be used as an adverb (*she is 4 feet 10 inches maximum*). Usage is similar for **optimum** and **optimal** (best, most favourable, most effective), and for **minimum** and **minimal** (smallest, least), though minimal can also be used to mean negligible (*minimal effort*) and in art and design to mean characterised by simple forms and lack of adornment, or minimalist.

**Maybe** is an adverb that means possibly, perhaps (*maybe you're just not ready*). **May be** is a possibility expressed in a different way in two words (*it may be the case that you go home on the train*). Maybe is also used as a noun, generally in the plural, for people or things that are uncertain (*they are all maybes at this stage*). (See **everyday**)

Even though it is the plural of medium, the **media** is generally regarded as singular and so takes a singular verb. When the word refers to a collection of individual journalists, use the plural verb (*the media came from all over the country and were catered for at the event*). The same goes for most collective nouns, such as team, group, family, audience, staff. Police, however, are generally regarded as plural.

**Mendacity** is the tendency to be untruthful, or mendacious. A **mendicant** is an individual from a religious order who lives by begging for money and food, or is a formal word for a beggar.

**Meretricious** means attractive in a flashy way but of little value, fake (*meretricious clickbait*). It rarely refers to its original meaning, relating to a prostitute, but still retains that element of moral judgment. **Meritorious** means deserving praise or reward, i.e. having merit.

**Metal** is any of a group of chemical elements or mixtures that are generally hard, malleable and conduct heat and electricity. Road metal is broken stone used for roading. Heavy metal is loud, strident, guitar-led rock music, or certain dense chemical metals. **Mettle** is resilience and determination particularly in the face of difficulties, courage, staying power, strength of spirit and resolve. To be on one's mettle is to be ready to do one's best.

A **meter** is a device that measures the use of something, such as electricity or the distance travelled in a taxi. A **metre** (US: meter) is 100 centimetres, 1/1000 of 1 kilometre, and the regular arrangement of syllables in lines of poetry. It's also the poetic arrangement of words by rhythm and syllable stresses, and musical rhythm determined by beats and notes.

**Miasma** [mee-az-ma] is a literary word meaning an unpleasant smell (*a miasma of odours*) or an unpleasant atmosphere (*miasma of woe*). **Milieu** [mil-yir] is a literary word for a social environment (*the intellectual milieu*).

To **militate**, generally followed by against, is to have a substantial effect on preventing (*militate against any quick solution*). To **mitigate** is to lessen in force or intensity (*mitigating circumstances*).

**Mill** and **mull** have a variety of meanings, but two verb uses can be confused. To **mill** about/around is what a collection of people do when they move in an unstructured way, wandering without purpose, perhaps ahead of an organised event. To **mull** over is to think about deeply over a period of time, as in response to a proposal or request. You don't want to write mull about.

Something that's **minuscule** is very small. The word also refers to lower-case letters (capital letters are **majuscule**). It's the spelling that's the problem. Minuscule, etymologically related to minus — i.e. less — has been spelled as miniscule for a century and has become an accepted spelling in some quarters. This is still to be avoided. If something is **miniature**, meanwhile, it is very small of its kind, or an object or image much reduced from what would be considered its usual size (*miniature pony*).

To **mooch** is to loiter or wander around without purpose, or to beg or try to get something free of charge, to freeload, or to borrow without the intention of paying it back. A mooch is someone who does these things.

To **schmooze** is to chat in an engaged way with someone, especially with the intention of social or career gain. A **smooch** is a kiss, especially a noisy or ostentatious one, or to kiss in this way.

**Moot**, in adjectival form, traditionally means arguable, subject to debate. As a verb it means to bring up for debate, and a moot is a discussion of a hypothetical case. However, in the US the word, apparently drawing on its 'academic exercise' aspect, now generally means of no practical relevance or significance, even among educated writers and readers. If confusion is anticipated, it may be preferable to use another word, such as debatable or inconsequential. **Mute**, of course, is unrelated, meaning to be expressed without speech, or to remove or block the sound from something. A person can be temporarily mute, if overcome by emotion, for example, but it is dated and offensive to use with a person who cannot speak. (See **nonplussed, disinterested, fulsome**)

**Moral** means concerned with principles of wrong and right, virtuous. The moral of the story is a principle or general truth. One's morals are one's habits of public conduct. **Morale** is the psychological state of an individual or group especially relating to confidence and enthusiasm (*the workforce had poor morale*).

To **moulder** (US: molder) is to decay, crumble. To **smoulder** (US: smolder) is to burn slowly, especially without a flame. Figuratively, it means to withhold expressing strong feelings. Best not to confuse these two.

**Mucous** means relating to, consisting of, or producing — from mucous membranes — that thickish secretion, **mucus**. (See **callous, loath**)

Reflexive pronouns — **myself, herself, himself, itself, oneself, yourself, ourselves, yourselves, themselves** — are useful, but easy to misapply. Use them when the object of your verb is the same as your subject (*I am* *teaching myself how to play guitar; she was enjoying herself watching their antics; you should feel free to fix yourself a snack; they found themselves with time to kill*). Reflexive pronouns can be used for emphasis or to focus back on the subject (*I can do it myself; she wanted to keep it for herself; she steeled herself for the interview; he himself had been to boarding school, but refused to let his children go*) or to make clear who the subject is (*her sister was late, so she drove her to the ferry* but *she drove herself to the ferry*). Don't use reflexive pronouns for everyday actions unless you want to emphasise the point that they did it alone (*the boy did it all by himself; she dressed and grabbed her bag* but *she dressed herself despite her injuries*). Don't hypercorrect by putting myself, herself or himself in place of me, her or him in simple sentences (*the gift was for myself* is wrong; *the gift was for me* is right) Write 'people like us', rather than 'people like ourselves'. (See **whom**)

# N

If you are **nauseated** you are experiencing nausea — feeling sick with the possibility of vomiting. If something is **nauseating** it causes the sufferer to be affected by nausea (*boats nauseate me*) or filled with disgust (*the animal cruelty nauseated him*). A thing that's **nauseous** makes you feel like you might vomit, be it raw sewage (*a nauseous stench*) or an ill-chosen outfit (*a nauseous combination*), or feel disgust (*the nauseous details of the murder*), though most dictionaries accept that it is also widely used to describe feeling sick. (See **ruined**)

To **needle** is to provoke, taunt or irritate (*needling his rivals*); or a goading remark or a UK term for a state of antagonism (*there's a bit of needle in the game*). To **wheedle** is to persuade or slyly negotiate using flattery (*wheedling and cajoling*).

**New-age** ideas are associated with non-mainstream thought. They might incorporate alternative health practices, occult beliefs and cultural behaviour. This usage, particularly by those outside of such a belief system, is often not meant as a compliment. New-age can also be used more neutrally (*a new-age vacuum cleaner*). **New-fangled** is a disparaging, and now dated, term for a version of something, such as a device, that is new and different but not necessarily better. (See **occult**)

The word **noisome** has nothing to do with being **noisy** (loud, full of noise, attention-seeking, conspicuously showy). It is etymologically related to annoyance and means disgusting, offensive, having a seriously unpleasant smell; obnoxious, unpleasant or objectionable.

The idea that the word **none** must take a singular verb because of the belief that it means not one is superstition. Not one demands a singular verb but none, which can also mean not any, can take a singular or plural verb depending on the sense of the sentence. (*none of the brigade were found guilty of the massacre; none of the survivors was willing to go home*).

**Nonplussed** is an adjective meaning to be so surprised and confused that one is unsure how to react. *Non plus* is Latin for not more, so nonplussed suggests being at a loss for words. A new usage, well developed in North America and spreading fast, however, is to regard the word as meaning unperturbed, indifferent, bored — almost its opposite (a classier version of 'meh', perhaps). This use looks to be taking over, so make your intentions clear. (See **fulsome**, **moot**, **disinterested**)

# O

The **occult** is a collection of magical, mystical and supernatural ideas and practices, e.g. witchcraft. If something is occult it is secret or hidden, or mysterious, or available only to a select few. In medicine, occult means without detectable symptoms (*occult infection*) or detectable only through special tests (*occult blood in faeces*). In astronomy one body can occult another (*the moon occulted Venus*).

If you are talking about a deity, **omnipotent** [om-nip-ə-tint) means having unlimited power, but it can have the lesser sense of simply great power (*an omnipotent ruler*). A deity — or the narrator of a book — who is **omniscient** [om-nis-see-ent] has complete awareness or understanding.

**Orotund**, said of the voice or speech, is full, strong, rich, clear. Said of speech or writing it is pompous or bombastic. **Rotund**, said of a person, is round or rounded in shape, chubby. Said of voice, it means marked by fullness of sound. **Otiose** is a formal word meaning superfluous, serving no useful purpose, futile (*the additions seemed otiose*). Its earlier sense of idle, lazy is now uncommon.

Often mixed up are **overestimated** and **underestimated**, especially in sentences such as 'The likely effect of online shopping on high street shops can't be underestimated'. This statement, on the face of it, is wrong. Of course the effect can be underestimated. The problem is twofold: the negative + under- confuses, but also can't here is being used to mean shouldn't. Most of the time the reader or listener will unconsciously correct the sense of the statement. Something that's likely to be underestimated is often larger or greater than you realise; someone who is likely to be underestimated is usually capable of achieving more than you expect. If they can't be underestimated, they have the potential to surprise (*Iceland's football team can't be underestimated*). If you suggest that someone is being overestimated, you are saying they are being regarded as more important or have more skill than they actually have; if something is being overestimated, it is being regarded as larger or more important than it actually is. To say that something can't be overestimated, you are saying it is very important or larger than most people think (*the impact of global warming can't be overestimated*). To minimise confusion, avoid using can't with either word.

If something is done **overtly** it is done openly, not secretly, meant to be seen. **Covertly** is the opposite, being done without being publicly disclosed or acknowledged. (See **disinformation**)

**Overweening** is excessive, overbearing (*overweening pride*). To **wean** is to accustom an infant or other baby mammal to an alternative food than its mother's milk. By extension, it is to free someone of something they have become dependent on (*he weaned himself off the drug*), and to be weaned on something is to be accustomed to something from a young age (*I was weaned on video games*).

**Pain** is physical or mental anguish; a pain is an ache. To take pains to do something is to go to some trouble. A **pane** is a sheet of glass, especially one set in a window or door; it's also a sheet of paper stamps.

A **pair** is a set of two; to pair is to group into twos. To **pare** is to trim, remove the skin or edges from. To pare down is to trim something in size or number.

A **palate** is a sense of taste or appreciation, of food or wine, or the roof of the mouth. A **palette** is a range of colours in painting, film, computer art, eye make-up etc. A **pallet** is a portable platform, usually wooden, for moving goods with a forklift. (See **canvas**)

To **pamper** is to indulge, spoil, provide special treatment to someone. To **pander** to someone is to gratify or indulge their sometimes less noble desires or tastes (*pandering to the masses*).

A **pang** is a sharp spasm of pain or strong emotion. A **ping** is a sharp, high metallic sound, an ultrasound signal to detect objects, or a digital signal to detect another computer. To ping is to make such sounds, or is an informal term for punishing an infringement, such as by a referee. A **pong** is an informal term for an unpleasant smell. A **prang** is an informal term for a minor vehicle accident. A **prong** is one of the pointed ends of a fork, a pointed branch of an antler, or one of the metal points of a plug that fit into a socket. A **tine** is one of the pointed ends of a fork, or the pointed branch of an antler.

When you are talking about the limits of things, **parameter** and **perimeter** can easily get muddled. The parameters of something (it's usually in plural) are its range or rules or limits of scope (*the parameters of the inquiry*). In technical contexts such as mathematics or statistics, a parameter is a numerical or other factor in a set that defines a system or its characteristics. A perimeter is the boundary of a closed geometric figure, and the boundary or periphery of a specific area (*fences enclose the perimeter of the property*). In basketball the perimeter is the area of the court beyond the three-point line, or sometimes the area not controlled by the defensive team. (See **enquiry**)

To **parlay** [par-lay] is an informal US word meaning to use money or success in a way that leads to further success (*she parlayed the book into a film deal*), or to turn an initial amount into a greater stake by gambling. Or it's a cumulative series of bets. A **parley** [pah-lee] is a discussion with an enemy. To parley is to talk in this way.

**Passed** and **past** are related and sound the same. Passed is a past participle of pass. Past is a noun, adjective, adverb and preposition. In many contexts they are differentiated by the verbs to have and to be (*she is past the age of worrying about such things; she has passed her years of anxiety; the time for diplomacy has passed; the time for diplomacy is now past; past experience suggested it might be a mistake, so he passed on the* *opportunity; a bill has been passed by Parliament, and it might have passed into history; if it was a piece of legislation that no one wanted and has now been repealed, it's past history; the past is the past, and those times have passed; the dangers were past; he drove past the orphanage; the protesters filed past*). In past times someone might have had more **pastimes**, not pasttimes — hobbies or pursuits that help to pass the time pleasantly.

To **patronise** (US: patronize) can be both a good thing to do and a bad one. If you patronise someone you are apparently being kindly towards them but are actually being superior: you act in a patronising way towards them. If you patronise an establishment, such as a neighbourhood restaurant, however, you go there frequently because you like it, presumably: you become a patron of it. On the same semantic track, you might patronise local arts shows; that is, support them financially or otherwise. (See **condescending**)

A **peak** is a summit, both of a literal pointed-top mountain or a figurative achievement (*past his peak; peak traffic; in peak fitness*). **Peaky** is an informal term meaning off-colour, sickly; or having noticeable high-pitched peaks in voices or music, i.e. **pitchy**. To **peek** is to take a quick look, a peek. To **pique** is to inspire interest in (*to pique one's curiosity*) or to hurt someone's pride (*she was piqued by his presumption*). Pique is irritation or wounded pride (*his pique was unbounded*).

To **pedal** is to push levers on bicycle, i.e. pedals, also the word for the foot controls in a motor vehicle. In medicine, pedal [pee-dal] refers to the foot. A **pedaller** — US pedaler — is one who propels a bicycle. To **peddle** is informal for to sell goods, or to sell an illicit drug or a stolen item. It also means to push a point of view (*peddle her ideas*). A **peddler** is someone who goes around selling goods, or someone who retails drugs. (See **licit**)

A **penchant** [pon-shont] is a strong liking for something or a habit of doing it, often for something negative (*a penchant for fast, expensive* *cars*). A **predilection** [pred-i-lek-shun] is an established preference. A **proclivity** [pro-cliv-i-tee] is a strong, established proneness, particularly to something objectionable. A **propensity** [pro-pens-i-tee] is an innate or deeply embedded tendency, often something regarded as negative, such as drinking too much or offering unwanted advice.

A piece of land that is almost surrounded by water or protrudes outward into water is a **peninsula**. The adjective is **peninsular** (*a peninsular part of the country*). Best to double-check your spelling on this.

**Perfidy** [pir-fi-dee] is a deliberate breach of faith or trust; treachery. **Perversity** [pir-vers-i-tee] is the quality or state of being contrary in nature or to what's expected, desired or reasonable. (See **treachery**)

To **persecute** is to pursue and harass a person or people, especially for their religious or political beliefs. To **prosecute** is to bring a legal case against a person or organisation; or a formal term for carrying on with legal or other action (*prosecuting a war*).

**Personal** [PIRS-ə-nil] means relating to a particular person, private, performed in person or done for a particular person (*personal favour*). A personal ad is a short advertisement expressing the relationship requirements of an individual. **Personnel** [pirs-ə-NEL] are the people employed in an organisation.

**Perspicacious** [per-spi-kay-shus] means being unusually perceptive and having solid and quick judgment in how things really are. The noun is perspicacity/perspicaciousness. It suggests wisdom and sensibleness.

A **poetaster** [poet-AS-tə] is an uncommon word for a person who writes inferior poetry. A **poet manqué** [mon-kay] is a poet who is frustrated or unfulfilled in achieving her or his aspirations. The term can be applied to other creative fields — artist manqué, journalist manqué. (See **crypto**)

A **pole** is a long, thin, rounded piece of wood or metal. It's also either extremity of the Earth's rotational axis, either of the ends of the axis of a sphere, either of two charged terminals of a battery or magnet, or either of diametrically opposed ideas (*poles apart*). A **poll** is a casting of votes in an election. To poll is to canvass in a survey.

**Politeness** is having or showing consideration or socially appropriate manners towards others. **Politesse** is formal or superficial politeness, gallantry. (See **complacent**)

That which is **politic** is marked by diplomacy, shrewd judgment or expediency (*a politic course of action*). To be unwise is impolitic. **Politicking** is engagement in political discussion or activity, usually to encourage others to back a particular party or candidate. **Polity** is the form or process of a society organised in a political way (*the country's democratic polity*). (See **comity**, **expedient**)

To **pontificate** is to pronounce self-importantly upon a subject. To **prognosticate** is to foretell.

**Poor** is without money or possessions, or the people who have little. To **pour** is to flow in a stream, or cause to flow, as of a drink. A **pore** is small passage in the skin. To pore over something is to study it intently. Don't write pour over something, which is to drench it.

**Portentous** means of large significance, as a portent or sign (*a portentous moment*); grave or serious (*portentous indications in the report*); or intended to impress or appear important (*portentous passages in a novel*). **Pretentious** means characterised by exaggerated ideas of importance or value (*a pretentious film*) or trying to appear smarter or notable than is warranted (*a pretentious theatre critic*).

**Posterity** means future generations (*the voyage was captured on film for posterity*). **Prosperity** means general wealth and success.

**Practicable** is feasible, capable of being put into practice or used. Its antonym is impracticable. **Practical** means useful, not theoretical, capable of being put to good use. Its antonym is impractical. **Pragmatic** means realistic, expedient and convenient. (See **expedient**)

To **pray** is to ask for or offer thanks to a deity or other object of worship, or to make a fervent wish for something. To **prey** upon someone or something is to victimise them, treat them as prey, or to exert a negative influence (*the thought preyed on his mind*).

To **precede** is to go before (*entertainment preceded the game*). To **proceed** is to go ahead, advance (*the match proceeded*).

Steepness is often described by two fancier words. **Precipitous** means steep or high, perhaps dangerously so (*precipitous slopes*), though it also means happening in a sudden and dramatic way (*a precipitous drop in the dollar*) and done rashly, i.e. too quickly without sufficient thought and planning (*a precipitous decision*). **Vertiginous** means very high or steep, that which might bring on vertigo or dizziness (*vertiginous roads wound through the canyon*) or applying to vertigo itself (*a vertiginous feeling overcame him*). It's taken on a new life in women's fashion, being used to refer to very high heels (*vertiginous stilettos*), which while they could break an ankle are unlikely to bring on the spins. (See **shear**)

A **premise** is a proposition forming the basis of a theory that helps to support a conclusion. **Premises** are a building and the grounds of a business (*no dogs allowed on the premises*).

**Prepossessing** means engaging or appealing in appearance (*not a prepossessing image*). Of an opinion, person etc., the rarer word

**prepossessed** means biased or prejudiced (*prepossessed of a notion*). Don't confuse it for **self-possessed**, which is calm, confident, composed (*grounded, self-possessed children*).

A **principal** is the head of an organisation or group, particularly a school; or a sum of money lent or invested as separate from the interest paid on it. A principal investigator is the highest in rank. A **principle** is a fundamental truth, law, moral grounding or assumption.

To **prise** (US: also prize) is to lever open or out. A **prize** is a reward or trophy, which is usually prized. To **pry** is to enquire in an intrusive or annoying way into someone else's life, to be nosy; or to lever something open or away from something else, usually by using a tool (*to pry open, loose, apart, away* etc.).

**Privation** is the condition or result of not having something, particularly basic necessities. **Probation** is a supervised non-jail period for offenders, or a trial period for new employees (*he was on probation*).

**Procrustean** means marked by the enforcing of conformity or uniformity, often ruthlessly, without regard for natural variation, individuality or special circumstances. Procrustes was a Greek villain of myth who killed his victims by forcing them to fit a bed by stretching them or cutting off the bits that overhung.

The biblical parable of the **prodigal** son is where many first heard the word. A father had two sons, the younger of whom went off and spent all his inheritance. Returning destitute, he was nonetheless welcomed back, much to his older brother's annoyance. The father told the older son he would inherit everything. Prodigal means spending in a wasteful and extravagant way. An allied meaning is providing or yielding on a lavish scale (*nature's prodigal bounty*). Because of the strong connection with the Bible tale, prodigal has gained a sense — often in the form of a prodigal son or daughter — of having departed from a usual place with the possibility or expectation of return. It is now recorded in dictionaries as a noun meaning both a person or group that is spendthrift (*the prodigals in council*), and someone who left and has returned (*the prodigal's return*). Use with care. (See **chagrin**)

A **prodigy** [pro-di-jee] is a young person of exceptional talents. **Progeny** [pro-jen-ee] is offspring or descendants, or the outcome or product of something (*the progeny of haste*). A **protégé** [pro-tay-zhay or proh-tə-zhay] is a talented young person who is mentored by a more experienced, prominent or influential person.

**Prone** is lying face downwards, or disposed towards something (*prone to gaining weight*). **Prostrate** is lying flat, face downwards and often with arms outstretched or completely overcome and perhaps unable to rise (*prostrate with grief*); or to lie or throw oneself flat on the ground in submission (*he prostrated himself*). In botany, prostrate plants grow along the ground (*a prostrate shrub*). The **prostate** is a gland in male mammals that releases the fluid component of semen. **Supine** means lying face upwards, or morally weak or unwilling to act or protest (*a supine regulator*).

If you have the ability to see into the future, or at least the belief that you can, the vision you describe is your **prophecy** [prof-is-ee] — and prophecy is your gift. What you do is **prophesy** [prof-is-eye].

**Prurient** means marked by an inordinate interest in sexual matters, particularly those of other people — prurience. **Pruritus** is a medical term for itching. The two words are related but don't confuse them.

A **pyrrhic** victory is won at such great cost that it can hardly be considered a victory. It doesn't mean a merely hard victory or an undecided result.

In physics, a **quantum** is the smallest indivisible amount or unit of something, such as energy; quantum mechanics is a theory of matter to do with subatomic particles. In everyday use, a quantum is an amount, a portion of something, especially one that is specified. Another sense has arisen, especially in adjectival use: that which is large or significant and unexpected, e.g. a quantum leap is a sudden and important advance.

To **quash** is to reject as invalid, particularly by legal action (*quashed the motion*) or to put a stop to (*quash closure rumours*; *quash a protest*). To **squash** is to squeeze or crush so that something becomes flattened, out of shape or into a small space, to reject or suppress. Squash is an indoor rackets game, a type of edible gourd or a drink made from concentrated fruit juice.

To **quiet** is to cause someone or something to be silent (chiefly US). To **quieten** is to make or become quiet or still (chiefly non-US). **Quietus** is a literary word for death or something that causes it, usually in relief; or a final settlement of a debt or obligation.

As an adverb, **quite** does a lot of work. It can mean completely, absolutely, to the greatest degree (*quite overwhelmed*; *quite the reverse*). Or as an intensifier, the equivalent of really or very (*quite amazing*; *quite a sight*). Or mean to some degree, the equivalent of fairly or pretty (*quite close to finishing*; *quite good*). It is frowned upon when used with an adjective relating to an absolute concept, such as unique, perfect, complete, infinite and equal. (See **unique**)

**Quixotic** means foolishly impractical or romantically idealistic, after the seventeenth century Spanish character, Don Quixote (*a quixotic political quest*). Another use of the word that's sneaking in and should be resisted is capricious or impulsive, as there is no shortage of synonyms for such behaviour.

**Rain** [rayn] is water falling from the sky. Or a heavy fall of something (*a rain of arrows*). To rain is to fall as or like rain (*ash rained down; shells rained down upon the troops*). It's worth noting that although **precipitation** is commonly used as a synonym for rain, to meteorologists hail, snow, sleet, drizzle, rain or **graupel** — snow pellets — is all precipitation. To **reign** [rayn] is to rule as a monarch; to be supreme in an area (*the game of AFL reigns in Australia*); to be the dominant emotion in a situation (*fear reigned during the attacks*). The period of time a monarch rules a country is her reign, as it is a period in charge for a boss (*his reign as manager of the club*). To **rein** in [rayn] is to restrain, direct or stop as with reins, the strap for the head of an animal. It has the wider sense of a restraining influence (*she kept a tight rein on her husband*) or controlling power (*assume the reins of government*). Write free rein and not free reign when you mean complete freedom to act.

To **raise** is to lift. To **raze** is to burn or level to the ground.

To **redact** is to edit or censor text, particularly by obscuring words or lines for legal, privacy or security reasons, as of an official document. To **retract** is to withdraw, as of an official statement or claim.

It is increasingly written that someone 'refutes' an outrageous — or possibly justified — claim made by someone else who has no fear of defamation lawyers. To **refute** is to disprove an argument or idea. To **rebut** is to provide strong evidence or a clear argument against. The intention in using refute to mean strongly deny or reject is probably to increase the apparent strength of the counterclaim, to signal success rather than an attempt. Even though this use of refute has been around for decades, careful users and traditionalists should push back on this for a while yet — or at least insist on less arguable terms like reject, deny, dispute, disprove. **Rebuff** means to, usually bluntly or rudely, reject or refuse, as of an approach; or a blunt rejection. **Rebuke** means to criticise sharply; or is a sharp disapproval. **Repudiate** means to deny or disclaim. To **debunk** an idea or notion is to show that it has less merit, substance or value than appears; to expose the sham nature of something.

Some traditionalists object to the word **relatable**. Its earlier meanings were able to be related, as of a story, or able to be related to something else, as of a process to result. It has recently taken on the meaning of 'able to relate to', as in empathise or identify with (*she is a very relatable person*). One objection is that most -able adjectives don't absorb a preposition. A translatable poem is one you can translate, a transportable box is one you can transport, but while you can relate a story, you relate *to* a person. Yet we accept other -able words that came across with a preposition: a compatible person is one you are compatible *with*; agreeable contract terms are those we agree *with*; a reliable plumber is one you can rely *on*; a laughable idea is one you can laugh *at*. Another objection to relatable is cultural: the insidious notion that every person or character needs to be someone we understand and are willing to empathise with. It assumes the qualities on offer are held by everyone, and discourages investigating the unfamiliar and potentially challenging. That's harder to defend. As is the word relatability. (See **insidious**)

**Reluctant** means averse, not willing, strongly hesitant (reluctant to give money); or assuming a role unwillingly (a reluctant suitor). It has negative connotations. A **reticent** person, by comparison, is reserved, taciturn, doesn't readily reveal her thoughts or feelings, or all that she knows. Inanimate objects, such as books or artworks, can also be considered reticent, in the sense of restrained. In recent years reticent has come to be used as a politer synonym for reluctant (*banks reticent to lend money*), perhaps because it lacks the wilful or predisposed sense of reluctant. It's wrong.

To **rend** is to tear something apart, literally (*the shark would rend the corpse into fragments*) or figuratively (*the discovery would rend the family*), or to cause great emotional or mental anguish to someone. It's often seen in literary contexts in its past form (*rent asunder*), or the adjectival rending (*a heart-rending story*). Don't confuse it with **render**, the meanings of which include providing something (*services rendered*), depicting (*beautifully rendered details*) or processing an image on a computer, or processing the carcass of an animal for its useful parts.

**Renown** [re-noun] is fame; **renowned** [re-nound] is famous.

To **resile** is to recoil or retract, to disavow, or to spring back into an original form. To be **reviled** is to be the subject of hateful abuse (*that movie producer was reviled*).

The word **restive** doesn't mean something that makes you want to rest, but almost the opposite — when applied to a person or people, it means restless, uneasy, difficult to control, impatient for something to happen. Applied to a horse it means unwilling to advance. The original, now obsolete sense was inclined to rest or remain still, but the shifting movements of a reluctant horse apparently contributed to the modern sense. (See **caustic**)

To **retch** is to vomit or make efforts to do so, or an act of vomiting. A **wretch** is an unhappy or unfortunate person, or an unpleasant or wicked one.

To **riffle** through the pages of a catalogue is to briefly and casually look at them. To **rifle** through a handbag is to look quickly but with determination, usually with the intention of stealing items of value.

**Right** is correct, or not left. To right is to correct. A right is an entitlement. A **rite** is a ceremonial observance. To **write** is to make letters or words, or to create software. A **wright** is a maker or repairer of things, usually in compounds, such as playwright.

**Risky** [ris-kee] means dangerous, involving the possibility of harm, embarrassment, failure or loss (*a risky venture*). **Risqué** [ris-kay] means bawdy, on the edge of decency, especially humour or talk of a sexual nature (*risqué jokes*).

A **root** is the part of a plant in soil, the base part of tooth or hair, a cause or origin, a mathematical number. To root around means to rummage; to root out means to expose and remove something objectionable. To **rout** is to defeat overwhelmingly and cause to flee, as an enemy. To rout out is to force out of hiding or gouge out. A rout [rowt] is an overwhelming defeat. A **route** [UK: root, US: often rowt] is a specified course or direction, method or process. To route is to send in a particular direction, as of internet traffic.

**Ruined** means destroyed, in a state of ruin, spoiled. **Ruinous** is occasionally used to mean destroyed, but more often means likely to cause ruin, whether physical, financial or other (*ruinous storm*; *ruinous choices*; *ruinous costs*). (See **nauseated**)

**Sank** is the past tense of sink, **sunk** the past participle (*they sank the boat*; *they have sunk many boats*). Likewise **shrank** and **shrunk** from shrink (*I shrank my overdraft, but I should have shrunk it earlier*). **Shrunken** is also used as a past participle and adjective (*a shrunken deficit*). **Sprang** and **sprung** come from spring (*I sprang a trap for her, because you have sprung too many that have failed*), and **stank** and **stunk** from stink (*she stank the place out with her cooking, not that I haven't stunk it out before*). It should be noted that **sat** is commonly used in general conversation in Britain when 'seated' or 'sitting' might be expected (*he was sat right where you are now*) and **stood** when 'standing' might be.

**Sarcastic** means expressing cutting ridicule or contempt, usually delivered ironically. **Sardonic** means mocking, scornful, sneering. **Satirical** means holding up human folly to ridicule. (See **ironic**)

To **scald** [skawld] is to injure with hot liquid or steam, or to immerse something in boiling water, such as food. A scald is an injury from boiling water. To **scold** [skold] is to tell someone off. A scold, in a dated and potentially offensive use, is a nagging or publicly grumbling person, usually a woman.

A **sceptic** (US: skeptic) is a person habitually inclined to question or doubt accepted opinions. **Septic** means infected with bacteria, rotting, unpleasant, nasty; a septic tank allows solid sewage to settle and decompose by way of anaerobic bacteria. Don't confuse the spelling.

**Schadenfreude** is pleasure had in others' misfortune. **Serendipity** is an instance or the development of making pleasant or fortunate discoveries by accident (*a serendipitous meeting*). **Synchronicity** is the simultaneous occurrence of events that appear to be linked but have no apparent causal connection, or simply simultaneous action.

To **scrimp** is to be sparing, especially in spending. To **skimp** is to carry out or supply insufficiently, almost always in the form skimp on.

To **sear** is to scorch or burn the surface of something, to fry meat quickly to keep in its juice, or to permanently mark or be experienced in a similar way as a burn. A **seer** is a person with claimed supernatural predictive abilities. **Sere** is literary for dry or withered.

**Sedation** is the act of administering a sedative drug to reduce anxiety or produce sleep, or the state of calm or reduced anxiety induced by a sedative drug. **Sedition** is revolt or incitement to resistance or insurrection against a government or lawful authority. (See **anaesthetic**)

A **segue** [seg-way] is a smooth transition from one discussion subject, film scene or piece of music to another. To segue is to make a smooth transition.

**Sewage** is waste in liquid or solid form in modern societies that's carried off in sewers or drains. **Sewerage** is the system of sewers and drains and removal of waste products. It's sewerage system but sewage treatment, pipes, works.

To **shear** is to remove the fleece or hair, typically of an animal. To shear off is to break off, as a wing on a plane. Shearing forces act on an object in two opposing directions. Wind shear is variation in wind speed and direction that concerns pilots. **Sheer** means vertical or nearly so, as of a mountain, with little indication of the drop beforehand; very thin or transparent, as in a stocking; or without qualification, exception or deviation (*sheer madness*). A sheer is a deviation, typically by a boat; to sheer away is to swerve from a course. (See **precipitous**)

A **shibboleth** was originally a particular use of language, such as a pronunciation, that identified someone as a member of a group — or not. It expanded, especially in North America, to encompass a language usage, custom or belief of a group of people, especially one that is now regarded by those outside as outdated or less important (*they cling to the old political shibboleths*). But it has spread further. Apart from the language use or custom it can also be that widely held belief past its use-by date or which probably can't be trusted, or a platitude, truism or catch-phrase. Use with care or opt for another word.

To **shimmer** is to flicker or sparkle. A shimmer is a soft, slowly flickering light. To **shimmy** is to shake one's shoulders and hips, especially in a dance, to feign a move to evade a tackler in a sports match, or to move without effort, glide (*shimmy into position*; *shimmy over*). A shimmy is also a light, abnormal shaking such as of a motor vehicle.

If something's a **shoo-in**, not shoe-in, it's a sure thing, a certainty, especially anything or anyone in a competition (*she's a shoo-in for CEO*). The term meant a certain winner (originally fixed) in horse racing, and derives from the sense of shoo-ing an animal, for instance, in a preferred direction.

**Silicon** is a grey, non-metal, semi-conducting chemical element often used in electronic circuits (*silicon chip*), alloys and steelmaking. As a result, we have California's Silicon Valley, and technology clusters in the US and around the world that model themselves on it: Silicon Allee, Silicon Hills, Silicon Cape, Silicon Gulf, Silicon Roundabout, Silicon Fen. **Silicone** is a compound of silicon, usually water-resistant, used for plastics, binders, polishes, lubricants, etc., and as the shell and sometimes inner material for breast implants.

Something that's **simple** is easy, uncomplicated, straightforward; or plain and unpretentious. If it's **simplistic** it's overly simplified, or treats something as simpler than it is (*simplistic thinking*). (See **complex**)

**Singular** can indicate uniqueness (*her singular vision*) or single (*it was a singular opportunity*), or mean exceptional or really good (*it was his singular good fortune*). It can also mean unusual or peculiar (*her singular sense of humour worried her lawyer*). Or in a grammar sense: 'the singular of geese is goose'. As a noun and verb, **signal** is clear enough — a sign, message, warning or similar that conveys information or directions, or the use of such signs (*hand signal; train signal; getting mixed signals from the boss*). Or information or an electrical impulse sent or received (*a radio signal*). But signal as an adjective means notable, distinguishable from the ordinary (*the signal importance of combating climate change*). (See **unique**)

To **skew** something is to turn at an angle and so distort, apply a bias (*a skewed view*) or change direction. A skew is a slanting or oblique direction, and skew means crooked. Don't confuse distortion with biting criticism. A **skewer** is a long solid rod to secure food on for cooking, food you skewer, but to skewer is also to subject to sharp criticism or ridicule.

To **slather** is to spread on thickly. Open slather means having complete freedom to act. To **lather** is produce a lather, a froth produced by mixing a soapy substance with water. Or to spread a thick layer on (*she lathered the piece of toast with butter*). A lather is a heavy, foamy sweat on a horse's coat, or a very agitated state (*he worked himself into a lather*). To **slaver** [slath-ah] is to slobber or drool; to slaver over someone is to fawn or show overzealous interest in (*he slavered over the guests*). Slaver is saliva running from the mouth. A slaver [slav-ah] is someone who is engaged in the trafficking of slaves. To **slobber** is to drool saliva, to slobber over someone or show excessive enthusiasm for. Slobber is saliva running from the mouth, drool.

**Soi-disant** is a fancy term from French that means self-styled, would-be (*England's soi-disant literary saviour*). Some traditionalists resist a newer use of so-called (*soi-disant psychic*) but this is now well established.

A **solecism** is a mistake in grammar, expression or etiquette. A **syllogism** is a form of reasoning that draws a conclusion from two premises which is not necessarily valid (*Dogs kill people. A spoodle is a dog. Spoodles kill people.*) or deductive reasoning in general. **Solipsism** is the view that one's self is the only knowable thing, or the quality of being extremely egocentric or selfish, i.e. solipsistic.

**Solid** is firm and solid, having three dimensions, not hollow or free from empty spaces, or continuous, undivided. Of a person, it's reliable. A **stolid** person is calm, dependable, incapable of being easily excited or animated. A **stoic** is someone who shows patient indifference to difficulty or pain without complaint, i.e. be stoic, derived from the ancient Greek philosophical school of Stoicism. (See **trouper**)

That which is **soporific** causes or encourages sleep. Soporific also means drowsy, or is a substance that causes sleep. That which is **sudorific** causes or induces sweat.

To **spatter** is to splash a liquid in small drops. A spatter is such splashing. To **splatter** is to cause a liquid to be spread on a surface in large drops, leaving a splatter or two. To **splutter** is to speak quickly and confusedly, as when experiencing strong emotion, or to spray droplets, as when speaking. Or to make spitting sounds, as a vehicle struggling to start, a splutter. To **sputter** is to make spitting or popping sounds, as an open fire; in physics, to sputter is to remove atoms from the surface of a solid or to coat a surface with atoms. A sputter is a spitting, popping noise. A **smattering** is a small amount, as of knowledge of a language or applause.

Is there a difference between a **stammer** and a **stutter**? Both mean the unfortunate involuntary repetition of sounds by sufferers, often initial consonants. The two are often used interchangeably, though stutter is probably more common in the US and stammer in the UK. Some people swear that the two terms refer to different maladies, that a stutter is the initial repetition and a stammer is the inability to complete a word, for instance, but specialist organisations don't differentiate. But while a car or a machine gun or an economy can stutter — that is, move forward in a faltering way — they can't stammer. (See **falter**)

Traditionally, to **stanch** is to stop the flow of, particularly blood. But **staunch** — otherwise having the sense of firm, steadfast, determined — is now used so often to mean stanch that it's probably the more common word.

**Stationary** means not moving. **Stationery** is writing materials. Another one worth double-checking the spelling.

A **statue** is a three-dimensional likeness of someone or something, most usually a person or animal. A **statute** is a specific law, in written form.

A **story** is an account of events, a tale or anecdote. In the US it is also a floor or level of a building. In some other countries a **storey** is a floor or level of a building (*a twenty-storey office block*). Something that's **storied** is celebrated or famous for having an interesting history, or is ornamented with scenes from history.

Something that's **straight** is without angle or curve or not askew; as well as not humorous, direct, ordered, undiluted, etc. A straight person is conventional, not evasive, heterosexual. A straight is a piece of a racecourse or road without bend, or sequence in cards. A **strait** is a narrow marine channel. In dire straits means in a very difficult situation. **Straitened** means restricted, or characterised by poverty (*straitened circumstances*).

**Substantial** means of considerable size, importance or worth, tangible, strongly made. **Substantive** means based on real facts and so important, meaningful, essential, independent, serious (*substantive argument*), independent. In law, it means creating and defining rights and duties.

**Systematic** means according to an organised plan, system or series of methods; methodical (*she was systematic in her audit*). **Systemic** means affecting an entire system, such as a human body, or relating to the whole of an organisation rather than just parts of it (*the bias was determined to be systemic*).

# T

**Tacit** means understood without being directly stated; inferred from or implied by actions or statements. To not be tacit is to be **explicit**.

To **tantalise** (US: tantalize) is to tease or torment with something appealing but keep it just out of reach, or to excite the senses (*the notion of universal healthcare is a tantalising prospect*). To **tanalise** is to treat wood with a mixture of chromium, copper and arsenic to prevent rot, from an earlier patent name. To **titillate** is to excite or stimulate pleasurably, especially using sexual images or language, though only to a minor degree (*done to titillate teenage boys*). To **titivate** is a less common word meaning to spruce up, make smart (*titivate the bedroom*; *titivated herself*).

**Taught** means instructed, educated. **Taut** is tightly drawn, under tension. A **tort** is a civil wrong under common law. **Rort** is Australian/ New Zealand slang for a dishonest scheme or fraud, or to defraud. A **torte** [taw-tə] is a type of rich, sweet cake. (See **tortious**)

To be on **tenterhooks** (not tender hooks) is to be kept in terrible suspense. A tenterhook — a fossil word that is probably only to be found in this phrase — is a hook that kept cloth on a frame for stretching, hence the idea of one's emotions being fully extended.

Much ink has been spilled over **that** and **which**. In the case of relative pronouns, that defines or limits what you are talking about (*this is the dog that bit me*). Which doesn't define but adds information. If more information is gained, you can use which (*it's the three dogs that bit me which will be put down*). If it's a relative clause — i.e. a comma is involved — it's usually which (*the dog, which bit me, was destroyed; each person came to the party with a bottle, which was put in the fridge*). Sometimes the use of that in a non-defining clause will simply sound wrong. 'The cook celebrated his groundbreaking dish that gave him the win in the final round' should be 'which gave him'. But this is right: 'The cook celebrated the groundbreaking dish that gave him the win in the final round.' And this: 'The hurt and harm created by the immigration purges introduced feelings of anger which never disappeared.' If the sentence is of a more formal style and involves a preposition, use which (*this is a topic about which much more will be said; it's a cause to which I will keep giving time and money*). Compare it with whom (*here is a man about whom we know very little*). In spoken English in particular, that is far more common outside of relative clauses. Always be aware of the possibility of dropping the pronoun, except where you can't. (Alien *is a film (that) I always watch at Christmas* but: Alien *is a film that always reminds me of Christmas*). One guide is that if you can't remove the information or put it inside commas or parentheses without making the sentence nonsense, use that. (See **whom**)

**Their** means of or belonging to them. **There** is not here. **They're** is the contracted form of 'they are'.

**Theology** is the study of religion and the nature of God. **Theosophy** is any of various doctrines of philosophical or religious thought that claim mystical insight can provide knowledge of God and the world. **Philosophy** is the rational study of truths, principles and problems of reality, existence, knowledge and conduct. **Taxonomy** is the science or technique of classification, particularly of forms of life. **Teleology** is the philosophical study of nature that attempts to describe things in terms of their apparent purpose; or belief that everything has a particular purpose or use.

**Throes** are spasms, struggles, severe pain (*death throes*), so the phrase 'in the throes of' means in the middle of something painful or unpleasant. All other meanings — throwing one's voice, light, a look, a fit, a punch, a party, a piece of pottery — are **throws**.

**Tinea** is one of several itching skin diseases caused by a fungus otherwise known as athlete's foot or ringworm. **Tinnitus** [tin-i-tus] is ringing or buzzing noise in the ears that doesn't come from external sources.

To **tire** is to get weary or cause to be tired, or to become bored with someone or something. A **tyre** in many parts of the word is the rubber outer rim of a wheel, which is spelled tire in the US.

**Tiresome** doesn't mean tiring, though a tiresome meeting might cause mental, if not also physical, fatigue. It means irritating, irksome, tedious, boring.

Those who **toe the line** agree to the policies and discipline of an organisation, often without complete willingness, the phrase coming from competitors starting from the same point. They don't tow the line, unless perhaps they are fishing.

Four words that ultimately come from Latin might be mixed up, particularly given the 't' start and the 'id' finish. **Torpid** means sluggish, apathetic, inactive, dormant. **Tumid** means swollen, inflated. **Turbid** is cloudy, muddy, opaque, as of a liquid or sky; or confused or muddled, as of feelings. **Turgid** means bloated (as of an organ), and excessively ornate or tedious (as of a piece of writing).

**Tortured** means pained, especially mentally. **Torturous** means causing torture or cruelly painful. **Tortuous** is often used instead of torturous, but means winding, not straightforward, devious. A Formula One track might be either or both. **Tortious** means having the nature of or involving a legal tort, or wrongful. (See **taught**)

Substances that can cause us harm are frequently interchanged, but they have precise technical meanings. A **toxin** is a substance that harms us — or other living beings — in small amounts (everything is toxic if the dose is large enough). A **poison** is a toxin that acts when ingested, inhaled or is absorbed through the skin. A **venom** is a toxin that arrives into our body by way of a wound created by the creature, i.e. a bite or sting. So snakes tend to be venomous and frogs poisonous to touch — though there are also poisonous snakes. A **toxungen** is a newish technical word for a toxin that is spat or squirted at a victim; a toxin tends to be produced by a living creature, whereas a **toxicant** is generally considered to be synthetic and introduced to the environment, such as a pesticide.

Trawling and trolling are sometimes confused, perhaps because there is some semantic overlap. To **trawl** is to catch fish, or attempt to, with a wide-mouthed net along the bottom of a body of water. It's also to search thoroughly in an attempt to find something or someone, or such a search. A **troll** has, until recent times, been an unattractive Scandinavian mythical creature, usually a giant but also a dwarf. But since the 1990s it is more commonly a person who makes deliberately provocative comments on social media to get a reaction — trolling. But trolling also means to fish by trailing a baited line behind a boat — plus the line or bait itself — as well as to extensively search in a number of places for something.

**Treachery** is betrayal of a person's faith or trust. **Treason** is the offence of trying to overthrow one's country or do harm to its sovereign — a person who commits treason is a **traitor**. (See **perfidy**)

A **trooper** is a mounted soldier or US state policeman; in the UK a trooper is a ship designed for carrying troops. A **trouper** is an entertainer or actor, particularly one with experience, perhaps from being in a travelling group or troupe; and so an experienced, dependable person, particularly one who doesn't complain about hardship (*a real trouper*). The term 'real trouper' is spelled as 'real trooper' probably at least as often in common use, but is still regarded by many as incorrect. (See **solid**)

If something is **unbearable** it is too bad, harsh or extreme to be able to be endured or tolerated. If it's **untenable** it is not able to be defended or maintained, such as an argument or point of view.

If a funeral procession is happening, is it under way or **underway**? The trend to making some terms into a single word is unstoppable, and this one should not be resisted.

Can something be very unique? No, say the traditionalists. **Unique** relates to an absolute concept, meaning one of a kind or unequalled, and there can be no gradations of uniqueness. Using very, absolutely, completely, somewhat, fairly, more or most is ridiculous. Hold on, say the dictionaries. Words like unique, perfect, complete, infinite and equal have a core mathematical meaning that's absolute and unqualifiable, but they often have less precise meanings. Unique has secondary meanings of characteristic, peculiar or connected to, usually in the form of 'unique to' (*the size and political power of the gun lobby is unique to America*), and remarkable, special or unusual (*a unique insight into premodern history*).

Says the Oxford Dictionaries website: 'In its secondary sense, unique does not relate to an absolute concept, and so the use of submodifying adverbs is grammatically acceptable.' Hard to see stalwarts won over by this. Such particularly strong feelings are held in this matter that *Cambridge Dictionary* recommends avoiding the use of more, most and very with unique 'when writing or speaking to people who are likely to be precise about the use of language'. (See **quite**, **singular**)

# V

**Vain** is excessively proud, especially of one's appearance, to indulge in vanity. **Vainglorious** means boastful, excessively proud of one's achievements. A **vein** is a blood vessel, particularly one that takes oxygen-depleted blood to the heart; a deposit or bed in rock containing desired minerals, and hence a metaphorical source (*a rich vein of comic material*); a distinctive mode of expression, quality or line of thought or action (*in that vein*); a vein-like wavy stripe of a different colour, particularly in marble, wood or cheese; a rib in a leaf or an insect's wings. An **artery** — also used metaphorically for vehicular, river or communication channels — takes oxygen-enriched blood away from the heart.

A **vale** [vail] is literary or historic for a valley. It's literary for the world, especially 'this vale of tears' from the Bible, referring to the sorrows of life. Vale [vah-lay] is an archaic expression of farewell. A **veil** is a piece of thin material worn by women to cover the face or head; or, often literary, something that conceals, disguises or makes something hard to understand; to cover or conceal as with a veil. Veiled means lightly disguised, especially as in 'a thinly veiled threat'.

**Venal** is open to bribery, corruptible (*venal politicians*). **Venial** means easily forgiven or minor, especially a moral transgression.

A **visit** is a temporary stay or a social call. A **visitation** is the appearance of a supernatural being; an official visit, for example, a senior church official to a diocese. It is also a catastrophe regarded as divine punishment (*visitation of an earthquake*), and in the US a gathering of a deceased person's family before a funeral. In legal contexts it's to do with an estranged parent's access to their children, or a spouse to a prisoner (*visitation rights*).

Said of an economic market or political situation, **volatile** means liable to change suddenly and unpredictably. Of a person it means prone to rapid mood changes, particularly anger or violence. Of a substance it means likely to evaporate at relatively low temperatures. A person who's **voluble** talks fluidly, easily and at length. Of speech it's fluid, confident and often forceful.

**Volition** is the act of making a conscious choice (*he left the party of his own volition*) or the power to choose (*she is able to exercise her volition*). **Volution**, a less common word, is a turning or revolving motion; a twist or single turn around a centre or a spiral; and in zoology, one of the whorls of a spiral gastropod's shell.

**Wacky** — occasionally spelled whacky — means oddly amusing or amusingly odd, silly, peculiar. To **whack** is to strike with a sharp and resounding blow, a whack. It's also US slang meaning to murder. Out of whack means to be not in working order.

To **wade** is to walk through water or other impeding substance, or to work one's way through something, such as a book. To wade in is to start to say or do something in a forceful manner, often without having thought carefully about it. To **weigh** in is to become involved in a debate or discussion in a forceful manner. Or to be officially weighed, as for a boxing match or in horse racing.

A **wage** is regular payment for work, but to wage is to engage in an activity, such as war. A **wager** is a bet of money on the outcome of an event or an agreement that one will take such a gamble. To wager is a dated expression meaning to offer one's opinion on the truth of something or the outcome of a future event (*I'll wager there'll be rain tomorrow*).

To **waive** is to give up a claim to something one would normally have rights to, or refrain from insisting on them (*she waived name suppression*). A **waiver** is an agreement or document demonstrating that a right has been waived, or the act of giving up a known right (*he signed the waiver*). A **wave** is a moving ridge of water on the sea etc., a shape or pattern like a recurring wave, or a sudden occurrence or rise (*a wave of panic*; *a wave of attacks*); a movement of the hand as a signal or greeting; in physics, a pattern in some kinds of energy; to move one's hand as a signal or greeting; to style hair with a slight curl; to move slightly in a fixed position (*flags waved in the wind*). To **waver** is to flicker, quiver (*the flame wavered in the breeze*), to vacillate between two choices, or to show or feel doubt (*the news caused her to waver*), to hesitate or falter (*his support never wavered*). (See **equivocation**)

To **wangle** is an informal term that means to obtain something or get to do something by being clever, often by persuasion or gentle manipulation of someone (*wangle a free ticket*; *wangle it so I can go*). A **wrangle** is a lengthy, often complicated argument or dispute, or to engage in one (*legal wrangling*; *ongoing wrangles with authorities*). But wrangle is increasingly used to mean obtain (*wrangled a pay increase*). It did have that meaning a few centuries ago but the sense was lost. Perhaps it has returned in confusion with wangle, or in collaboration with the North American sense of wrangling horses — that is, herding them. Best to make your intentions clear.

The current or near-future state of meteorological conditions in an area is the **weather**. The meteorological conditions that prevail in an area over a long period are its **climate**. **Whether** means if, in case. A **wether** is a castrated ram.

**While** means during, at the same time (*while you were sleeping*); or to pass time (*while away the hours*). Avoid **whilst**, which is an attempt to be literary. Take care using while as a preposition instead of and, although, whereas, given its primary meaning of 'at the same time'. **Wiles** is literary for charm or cunning (*feminine wiles*).

**Whom** shouldn't be feared. The object form of who is uncommon except in formal writing or speaking, and — to be blunt — usually can be replaced by who without fuss. Most people will be familiar with its use when combined with a preposition (*To whom are you speaking? For whom are you doing this task? With whom are you going? This is being produced by whom?*). A useful rule of thumb is to flip the sentence around and look for whether 'who' refers to the subject or object of the sentence, noting that whom replaces him, her, them, it (noting the m ending of him or them might be easiest). So: Whom should I address this to? This is correct, because you address it him/her/them. Who did this? She did this. It's important to note that sometimes whom sounds too fussy even for careful users. Many will prefer: Who was the book about? It should properly be whom, as it was about them. Similarly: You nominated who for the job? Even though you nominated her or him. If there's another verb present in the sentence, who is more likely: I nominated the person who was best qualified — because she was best qualified. Or: I voted for the person who shared my views — he shared my views. Don't get caught up in hypercorrection. 'Whomever thinks this, is silly' is wrong, because they/she/he thinks it, not them/her/him. 'Whomever I want to go will be chosen' is correct, if fussy, because I want them to go. 'I can give it to whomever I like' is correct, because I can give it to them, though again fussy. 'Whomever I think is worthy will go' is wrong, because I think they are worthy. 'The trial lawyer, whom he knew was fierce, began her argument' is wrong, because he knew she was fierce. But: 'The trial lawyer, whom he knew to be fierce, began her argument' is right, because he knew her to be fierce. Note that phrases like 'I think' in sentences are effectively in parentheses: 'These are excellent players who I think should get a run' is correct, as who is not the object. I think they should get a run. 'These are excellent players whom we will give a run' is correct, because we will give them a run. If you are still unsure of the sentence or it sounds clunky, recast it to avoid who or whom altogether. (See **adieu, myself, that** and **which**)

A **wraith** is a supposed ghost or visible spirit, especially of a person around the time of their death. **Wrath** is extreme vengeful anger. A **wreath** is a ring of flowers or greenery, placed on someone's head or used as a commemoration or decoration.

To **wreak** is literary for bringing about or causing violent damage or harm (*to wreak havoc in society*); to inflict, particularly vengeance (*wreak her revenge*). To **reek** is to smell strongly and usually unpleasantly of something. To **wreck** is to ruin, spoil, badly damage something. It's a vehicle, such as a car or train, that has been in a severe crash, a shipwreck, or a person who is in poor physical or mental condition. If you hear the expression 'wreck havoc', it's incorrect. (See **fraught**)

# Unusual plurals

Words with irregular plurals generally change their endings like this:
-a = ae, -au = -aux, -ex/-ix = -ices, -is = -es, -ion = -ia, -on = -a, -o = -os
or -oes, -um = -a, -us = -i

agendas (from agenda), agents provocateurs (from agent provocateur),
algae ([al-ghee or al-jee] from alga, uncommon), alumnae (from
alumna), alumni (from alumnus), analyses (from analysis), appendices
(from appendix of a book), appendixes (from appendix taken out by a
surgeon), armadillos, attorneys general, avocados, axes (from axe, or ax
in US), axes (from axis, as in Axis of Evil)

bacteria (from bacterium), banjos or banjoes, beer or beers (four
bottles of beer, though four beers is common if informal, but beers of
the world), bimbos, bison, bistros, bongos, bonobos, brothers-in-law,
buffalo, bureaux or bureaus (from bureau)

cacti (from cactus), casinos, cellos, chateaux or chateaus (from chateau),
children (from child), cognoscenti (from cognoscente), commandos,
corpora or corpuses (from corpus, a body of written texts), courts
martial (from court martial), crises (from crisis), criteria (from
criterion), culs de sac (from cul de sac), curricula or curriculums (from
curriculum)

data (from datum, uncommon), daughters-in-law, deer, diagnoses (from diagnosis), dice (from dice or die), dildos, dingos, discos, dwarves (from dwarf)

echoes, egos, ellipses (from ellipsis), elves (from elf), embargoes, embryos, espressos, euros

feet (from foot), fiascos, fish or fishes (lots of fish but fishes of Australia), foci (from focus), fomites (from fomes, fomite), formulas or formulae (from formula), forums, occasionally for (from forum), fowl, fungi (from fungus)

gateaux or gateaus (from gateau), gazebos, geckos, geese, gigolos, governors general, graffiti (from graffito or graffiti), gymnasiums (gymnasia)

halves (from half), hippopotamuses, hoofs (or hooves), hors d'oeuvres (from hors d'oeuvre)

indexes (from index of a book), indices (from index of share prices), innuendoes

knives (from knife)

leaves (from leaf), lice (from louse), lives (from life, but still lifes), loaves (from loaf), loci (from locus)

manifestos, matrices (from matrix), maximums or maxima (from maximum), media (from medium, a channel of communication, type of information storage or particular environment), mediums (from medium, the spiritual kind or clothing size), mementoes, men (from man), mice (from mouse, but computer mouses), millennia (from millennium), mongooses, mosquitoes nachos, neutrinos, noes (from no), nuclei (from nucleus)

octopuses, offspring, oxen (from ox)

paninis, paparazzi (from paparazzo), passersby (from passerby), patios, people (from person), phenomena (from phenomenon), pianos, placebos, plateaus or plateaux (from plateau), potatoes

quanta (from quantum), quorums or quora (from quorum)

radii or radiuses, ratios, referendums or referenda (from referendum), roofs (from roof)

salmon, salvoes, scarves (from scarf), scissors, series, sheep, species, stadiums or stadia (from stadium), sties (from sty), stilettos, strata (from stratum), stimuli (from stimulus in scientific contexts), stimuluses (from economic stimulus), syllabuses (from syllabus)

teeth (from tooth), terminuses or termini (from terminus), theses (from thesis), tomatoes, tongs, torpedoes, trousers, trout, tuna, tuxedos, typos

ultimatums

vetoes, virtuosos or virtuosi (from virtuoso), volcanoes

weirdos, wives (from wife), wolves (from wolf), women (from woman)

yesses or yeses (from yes)

zeroes

# Clichéd 'streets'

the Arab street — supposed popular public opinion, particularly on
    political matters, in Arab countries or communities
Civvy Street — everyday civilian life, as opposed to, in particular, life in
    the armed forces (UK)
easy street — a comfortable and secure existence, particularly financially
Fleet Street — the British press
Grub Street — literary hacks (UK)
high street — generic city shopping precinct (UK)
K Street — home of US government lobby groups in Washington DC
Madison Avenue — US advertising world
Mahogany Row — generic corporate boardrooms
Main Street — the central street of a small town, metaphor for Middle
    America (US)
Millionaires' Row or Mile, Golden Mile — exclusive residential
    neighbourhoods of cities around the world
Queer Street — in debt or great difficulty (UK)
skid row — a squalid area of a city; severe difficulty, especially extreme
    financial hardship (US)
Struggle Street — everyday hardship (Australia & NZ)
Think Tank Row — home of many thinktanks in Massachusetts Avenue,
    Washington DC (US)
Tin Pan Alley — place of popular music production in New York city in
    late nineteenth and early twentieth century music
Wall Street — US stock exchange and financial centre

# Common social media abbreviations

Usage varies between capitals or lower case; style below attempts to duplicate generally more common.

AFAIK — as far as I know
AMA — ask me anything
ASL — age, sex, location
b4 — before
bc, b/c — because
bfn — bye for now
brb — be right back
btw — by the way
cc — carbon copy = a way to attempt to bring a potentially relevant tweet to someone's attention, when followed by a person's handle, such as @POTUS
cx — correction
dae — does anyone else ...
fml — fuck my life = used to express frustration or disappointment with events, often after a depressing statement
FOMO — fear of missing out
FTFY — fixed that for you = here's a solution; can be used ironically
FTR — for the record
ftw — for the win = used to celebrate a success
HMU — hit me up = let me know on this topic
h/t — hat-tip = polite acknowledgement of the source of something

IANAD — I am not a doctor

IANAL — I am not a lawyer

ICYMI — in case you missed it

idk — I don't know

ikr — I know, right?

IMO/IMHO — in my opinion/in my humble opinion

IRL — in real life

JK — just kidding

JSYK — just so you know = FYI — for your information

LMAO — laughing my ass off

LMK — let me know

lol — laughing out loud

lulz — (for) kicks

NSFW — not safe for work = potentially offensive

OH — overheard

ORLY? — oh really?

RT — retweet

SMH/SMDH — shaking my head/shaking my damn head

tbh — to be honest

TFTF — thanks for the follow

tfw — that feel(ing) when = used to describe an emotional reaction to
an experience either good or bad

TIA — thanks in advance

TIL — today I learned . . .

TL;DR — too long; didn't read = a piece is long and/or complicated,
and might indicate that a short summary follows

TMB — text/tweet/tag me back

ttyl — talk to you later

ty — thank you

w/ — with

wtf — what the fuck?

wtv — whatever

YMMV — your mileage may vary = this is what I found, though you
    may find something slightly different
YOLO — you only live once
YW — you're welcome

# Often misspelled

abattoir, aberrant, abscess, absence, abyss, academic, acceptable, access, accolade, accommodate, accommodation, accompany, according, accumulate, accuse, ache, acknowledge, acquaintance, acquire, acquit, across, address, adequate, adjacent, admissible, adolescence, adrenalin, advantageous, advertisement, advice (n), advise (v), adviser or advisor, aesthetic (US: also esthetic), affect (have an effect on), affidavit, affinity, aficionado, aggravate, aisle, algorithm, allegory, alliteration, allocation, almost, alphabet, altar (in a church), alter (to change), aluminium (US: aluminum), amateur, ambiance, anaesthetic (US: anesthetic), analyse (US: analyze), analysis, aneurysm, annihilation, anomalous, answer, Antarctic, antediluvian, antic, antidote, anxiety, apocryphal, apology, apostasy, apparel, arctic, assassination, assonance, asthma, asylum, atheist, attendance, autumn, auxiliary, awkward, axolotl

bachelor, barbecue (but BBQ), bassinet, battalion, beautiful, beginning, beleaguered, believe, bellwether, beneficial, benefited, benefiting, bicycle, bouillon, braggadocio, broccoli, bureau, burlesque, business, bused (US: also bussed), buses (US: also busses)

caesarean (US: cesarean), cafeteria, caffeine, caipirinha, calendar, camaraderie, camouflage, campaign, candour (US: candor), cannabis, capsize, Caribbean, cartilage, caster (one who casts), castor (wheel, sugar), catalogue (US: catalog), category, caterpillar, ceiling, cemetery, census, centenary, chameleon, chamomile, changeable, charlatan, chauffeur, chiaroscuro, chilblain, cholesterol, chrysalis, chutzpah, cigarette, coherent, collateral, collectible, colossal, colosseum, colour (US: color), column, comeuppance, commiserate, committed, committee, compliment, concede, conceive, condemn, condescension, confectionery, connoisseur, conscience, conscientious, conscious, consensual, consensus, convenience, corralled, correspondence, correspondent, coruscate, councillor (US: also councilor), counsellor (US: also counselor), courageous, curiosity, curriculum, cylinder

daiquiri, debutante, deceased, deceive, decrepit, deficient, definite, delinquent, delirious, demagogue, denouement or dénouement, dependant (n) (US: dependent), dependent (adj), descendant (n), descendent (adj), descent, desert (of sand), desiccated, desperate, dessert (of ice-cream), deteriorate, detriment, device (n), devise (v), diaphragm, diarrhoea (US: diarrhea), dichotomy, dilapidated, dilemma, dilettante, delirious, diocese, disastrous, disciple, discipline, discovery, discreet (careful and reliable), discrete (separate), discuss, disease, dishevelled (US: disheveled), dissatisfied, dissemble, dissension, dissipate, doesn't, doggerel, dominant, drunkenness, dumbbell

echoes, ecstasy, eczema, effect (outcome), effervescence, effervescent, efficient, eighth, eligible, eloquent, embarrassment, emissary, emphasise (US: emphasize), emphysema, encyclopedia, enormous, enough, enrol (US: enroll), ephemeral, epiphany, epistemology, epistle, equable, equivalent, especially, euthanasia, exaggerate, exceed, excruciating, exercise, exhibition, exhilarate, exhilaration, existence, exorbitant, expat(riate), expeditious, extravagant, exuberant

facetious, facsimile, faeces (US: feces), fascinate, feasible, February, fictitious, fiery, finesse, flamboyant, fluorescent, focusing, foetus, foreign, foreword, forgo, formally, formerly, forward, fossick, fourteen, fourth, frangible, frivolous, fulfil (US: fulfill), funeral, funereal, fusillade gaiety, gateau, gauge, genealogy, genuflect, genesis, genuine, glamorous, glamour (US: glamor), government, governor, graffiti, grammar, grandad, grandeur, grateful, grief, grievous, guarantee, guttural

haemorrhage (US: hemorrhage), handkerchief, hangar (for plane), hanger (for clothes), harassment, height, heinous, hiccup, hierarchy, high-jinx, hindrance, homonym, hors d'oeuvre(s), humiliate, humorous, humour (US: humor), hygiene, hypochondria, hypocrisy, hypocrite, hypoglycaemic (US: hypoglycemic)

idiosyncrasy, idiosyncratic, ignominy, ignorance, immense, inauguration, incandescence, increase, independent, indictment, indigenous, indispensable, ingenious, innocuous, inoculate, insistence, insouciance, instalment (US: installment), intercede, intermittent, interruptible, inure, inveigle, irascibility, iridescence, irrelevant, irresistible, irreverent, island

January, jealous, jeroboam, jewellery (US: jewelry)

kaleidoscope, ketchup, kindergarten, knick-knack (US: knickknack and also nicknack), knowledge

labelled (US: labeled), laboratory, labyrinth, lachrymosity, lacklustre (US: lackluster), language, largesse (US: also largess), larynx, leisure, leukaemia, liaison, library, licence (n), license (v; n, v in US), lieutenant, lightening (of a load), lightning (in the skies), linchpin, lovable (also loveable), lugubrious, lustre (US: luster), luxuries

maintenance, manoeuvre (US: maneuver), manufacture, marijuana, marriage, martyr, mausoleum, mayonnaise, medieval, mediocre, Mediterranean, memento, metropolitan, millennium, miniature, minuscule, miscellaneous, mischief, mischievous, misogyny, misspelled, moccasin, mollusc (US: mollusk), mosquito(es), muscle, mysterious necessary, neighbour (US: neighbor), niece, nonchalance, noticeable, nuclear, numerous

obsession, obsolescence, obstacle, obstreperous, occasion, occurrence, octopus, odyssey, oleaginous, omelette (US: omelet), onomatopoeia, ophthalmologist, oscillation, outrageous

panache, pandemonium, panorama, pantomime, paraffin, parallel, paralyse (US: paralyze), paraphernalia, parlour (US: parlor), parquet, pastime, pejorative, perceive, perennial, perseverance, persiflage, persistence, personal (of a person), personnel (staff), persuade, persuasion, perturb, pharaoh, pharynx, phenomenon, philosophy, physical, physics, piece, pigeon, pilgrimage, piranha, Pisces, pixelated (UK: also pixellated), playwright, plenary, plenitude, plough (US: plow), pneumatic, posthumous, practice (n; n, v in US), practise (v), prairie, precede, precedent, predilection, preferred, prejudice, premier (adj = high-status; n = head of state), premiere (n = first night of a performance), presence, pretence (US: pretense), previous, primeval, principal (of a school), principle (of philosophy), privilege, proceed, profited, program (UK, NZ if not software, then often: programme), propaganda, propagation, proprietor, proselytise (US: proselytize), protagonist, psoriasis, psychiatrist, psychology, publicly, pulleys, pumpkin, pusillanimity, pyjamas (US: pajamas), pyrrhic

qualities, quantum, questionnaire, quixotic, quorum

raccoon, rancour (US: rancor), raspberry, razzmatazz, realise (US: realize), receive, reconnaissance, referee, reference, regrettable, relieve, religion, religious, reminisce, renaissance, renown (n), renowned (adj), repetition, restaurant, restaurateur, resuscitate, reverend, rheumatism, rhyme, rhythm, righteous, rivalry, rococo saccharine, sacrilege, sacrilegious, salubrious, satiety, saucer, schedule, science, scissors, secretary, seize, sentence, separate, septicaemia (US: septicemia), sergeant, siege, silhouette, sincerely, skiing, skilful (US: skillful), skulduggery, sleigh, sleight, smoulder (US: smolder), sobriquet, solecism, solemn, solipsistic, souvenir, sovereignty, special, spontaneity, sprezzatura, squalor, squirrel, staccato, stationary, stationery, straighten, straitjacket, straitlaced, storey(s) (of a building) (US: story/stories), strength, strenuous, submerged, subtle, subtleties, succumb, sufficient, summary, supersede, supervisor, suppress, surprise, susceptible, suspense, suspicious, susurrate, sycophant, syllable, syllogism, symmetrical, symmetry, synonymous

tarpaulin, technique, tectonics, temperament, temperature, tenement, theatre (US: theater), thieves, thoroughfare, thought, threshold, throughout, toboggan, tourniquet, tragedy, transferred, tremendous, trespass, truly, tutelage, twelfth, twelve, typical, tyranny

unbelievable, unconscious, unctuous, undesirable, unmanageable

vacuum, valleys, vaudeville, vengeance, ventilate, ventriloquism, verisimilitude, veteran, vicinity, vicissitudes, viewing, vulnerable

waive, wealthiest, Wednesday, weird, wield, whenever, wherever, whether, whizz, wilful (US: also willful), witnessed, woollen (US: woolen), wrench

xenophobia, xylophone

yacht, Yahtzee, Yahweh, yarmulke, yawn, yield, yoghurt (UK: also yogurt, yoghourt), you're, yours

zabaglione, zealot, zealotry, zeugma, Zeus, zinc

# Bibliographical sources

Many language books, style guides and dictionaries have informed *Word to the Wise*, including the likes of Fowler and Partridge, and Kingley Amis's archly sticklerish *The King's English*. Like anyone interested in language, I have shelves of word books, including a highly combustible complete set of the 1933 *OED* (I also have a 2009 digital version). If I reach for a hardback dictionary it's usually *The Chambers Dictionary*, 12th Edition (2011) or *Chambers 20th Century Dictionary* (1983); in search of synonyms it might be the *Bloomsbury Thesaurus* (1993). Most often, unsurprisingly, I open browser tabs for the magnificent oxforddictionaries.com, merriam-webster.com, macmillandictionary. com, chambers.co.uk and dictionary.cambridge.org. The community-enabled wordnix.com, urbandictionary.com and powerthesaurus.org have also been helpful, particularly in tracking evolving meanings.

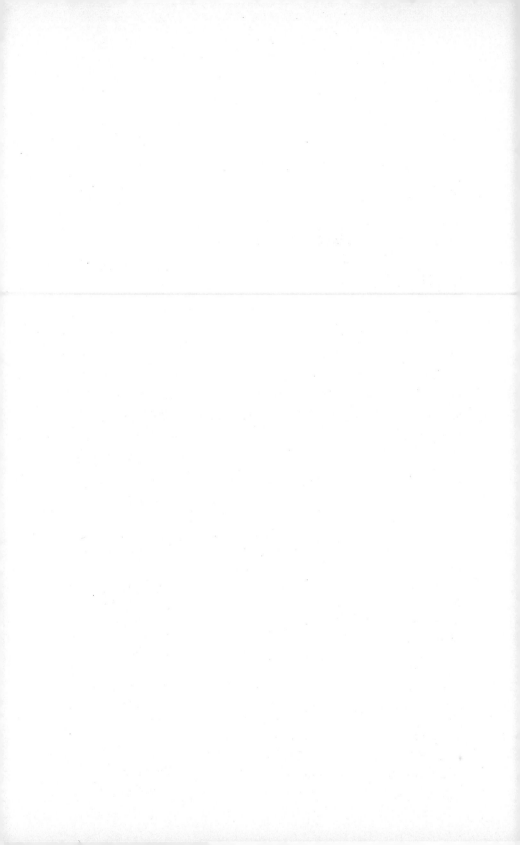

# Index

**Y**